The
COMPANIONS *in Christ*®
Network

www.companionsinchrist.org

So much more!

Companions in Christ offers *so much more* than printed resources. It offers an ongoing LEADERSHIP NETWORK that provides:

➤ Opportunities to connect with other churches who are also journeying through the *Companions in Christ* series.

➤ Helpful leadership tips and articles as well as updated lists of supplemental resources

➤ Training opportunities that develop and deepen the leadership skills used in formational groups

➤ An online discussion room where you can share or gather information

➤ Insights and testimonies from other *Companions in Christ* leaders

➤ FREE *Companions in Christ* posters to use as you promote the group in your congregation

Just complete this form and drop it in the mail, and you can enjoy the many benefits available through the Companions in Christ NETWORK! Or, enter your contact information at www.companionsinchrist.org/leaders.

☐ Add my name to the *Companions in Christ* NETWORK email list so that I can receive ongoing information about small-group resources and leadership trainings

☐ Please send me FREE *Companions in Christ* posters. Indicate quantity needed: (Also available online.)

Name: _____

Address: _____

City/State/Zip: _____

Church: _____

Email: _____

Phone: _____

COMPANIONS *in Christ*®

Upper Room Ministries
PO Box 340012
Nashville, TN 37203-9540

Leader's Guide, Revised Edition

COMPANIONS *in Christ*

A Small-Group Experience in Spiritual Formation

Stephen D. Bryant | Janice T. Grana
Marjorie J. Thompson

UPPER ROOM BOOKS®

NASHVILLE

COMPANIONS IN CHRIST
Leader's Guide
Copyright © 2006 by Upper Room Books®
All rights reserved.

The Upper Room® Web site http://www.upperroom.org

Unless otherwise stated, scripture quotations are from the New Revised Standard Version Bible, copyright © 1989 by the Division of Christian Education of the National Council of the Churches of Christ in the U.S.A. Used by permission. All rights reserved.

"The Broken Places," by Beth Richardson in *alive now!* (May/June 1991). Used by permission of The Upper Room.

Excerpt from a lecture given by Henri Nouwen at Scarritt-Bennett Center (February 8, 1991). Used by permission of the Henri Nouwen Literary Centre.

Excerpt from "The Pastor as Spiritual Director" by Roy W. Fairchild in *Quarterly Review* Vol. 5, no. 2 (Summer 1985), 32. Used by permission.

Cover design: Left Coast Design, Portland, OR
Cover photo: Scott Barrow Photography
First printing: 2006

Library of Congress Cataloging-in-Publication
Companions in Christ: leader's guide: a small-group experience in spiritual formation / Stephen D. Bryant...[et al.].
    p. cm.
    Includes bibliographical references.
    ISBN 0-8358-9840-7
    1. Spiritual formation—Study and teaching. 2. Small groups—Religious aspects—Christianity—Study and teaching. 3. Church group work. I. Bryant, Stephen D.
BV4511 .C553 2006
253.'7—dc21   00-043529

Printed in the United States of America

For more information on *Companions in Christ*
call 800-972-0433 or visit www.companionsinchrist.org

Contents

Acknowledgments

Companions in Christ is truly the result of the efforts of a team of persons who shared a common vision. The team members graciously contributed their knowledge and experience to develop a small-group resource that would creatively engage persons in a journey of spiritual growth and discovery. The authors of the weekly readings in the Participant's Book(s) were Gerrit Scott Dawson, Adele Gonzalez, E. Glenn Hinson, Rueben P. Job, Marjorie J. Thompson, and Wendy M. Wright. Stephen Bryant was the primary author of the daily exercises and the Leader's Guide. Marjorie Thompson created the original design and participated in the editing of the entire resource. Keith Beasley-Topliffe served as a consultant in the creation of the process for the small-group meetings and contributed numerous ideas that influenced the final shape of the resource. In the early stages of development, two advisory groups read and responded to the initial drafts of material. The persons participating as members of those advisory groups were Jeannette Bakke, Avery Brooke, Thomas Parker, Helen Pearson Smith, Luther E. Smith Jr., Eradio Valverde Jr., Diane Luton Blum, Carol Bumbalough, Ruth Torri, and Mark Wilson. Prior to publication, test groups in the following churches used the material and provided helpful suggestions for improvement of the Participant's Book and the Leader's Guide.

First United Methodist Church, Hartselle, Alabama
St. George's Episcopal Church, Nashville, Tennessee
Northwest Presbyterian Church, Atlanta, Georgia
Garfield Memorial United Methodist Church, Pepper Pike, Ohio
First United Methodist Church, Corpus Christi, Texas

Acknowledgments

Malibu United Methodist Church, Malibu, California
First United Methodist Church, Santa Monica, California
St. Paul United Methodist Church, San Antonio, Texas
Trinity Presbyterian Church, Arvada, Colorado
First United Methodist Church, Franklin, Tennessee
La Trinidad United Methodist Church, San Antonio, Texas
Aldersgate United Methodist Church, Slidell, Louisiana

My deep gratitude goes to all these persons and groups for their contribution to and support of *Companions in Christ*.

—Janice T. Grana, editor of *Companions in Christ*
April 2001

Weekly Needs at a Glance

To help you in your weekly preparation, here is a complete list of items needed for each of the weekly meetings.

ITEMS SUGGESTED FOR ALL MEETINGS

- Christ candle (large white pillar candle) or other central candle and cloth for worship table
- Hymnals, songbooks, or other arrangements for music
- Extra Bibles
- Group ground rules developed during your Preparatory Meeting and/or Covenant created in Part 1, Week 5
- Candle Prayer printed on newsprint
- Newsprint and markers
- *Optional*: Symbol on worship table for link with a partner group

PREPARATORY MEETING

- Participant's Book for each member
- Scripture text for opening worship (such as, Isaiah 40:3-5 or Mark 1:1-3)
- Paper and pencil for each participant
- *Optional*: A list of suggested study Bibles (page 233)
- Blank nametags and markers

PART 1 EMBRACING THE JOURNEY: THE WAY OF CHRIST

Week 1: The Christian Life As Journey
- Blank nametags and markers
- Handout for each participant on Ephesians 4 (page 37)

Week 2: The Nature of the Christian Spiritual Life
- Blank nametags and markers
- A bowl of water
- Handout for each participant on Mark 1:9-11 (page 45)
- Newsprint with the following, "_____, you are beloved, precious child of God and beautiful to behold!"

Week 3: The Flow and the Means of Grace
- Newsprint divided into three columns labeled "Prevenient," "Justifying," and "Sanctifying Grace"

Week 4: Sharing Journeys of Faith
- No additional materials required

Week 5: Living As Covenant Community
- Card from back of Leader's Guide, "Prayers for Our Companions in Christ Group"

PART 2 FEEDING ON THE WORD: THE MIND OF CHRIST

- List of churches taking *Companions in Christ* as found on the CIC Web site
- A card to sign or write personal greetings

Week 1: Why Do We Call the Bible God's Word?
- Handout for each participant, The Spirit of the Lord reflection sheets (pages 65–66)

Week 2: Studying Scripture As a Spiritual Discipline
- No additional materials needed

Week 3: Meditating on the Word
- Songbooks with Amy Grant's song, "Thy Word Is a Lamp unto My Feet" or an audiocassette or CD with the music or another hymn selection

Week 4: Directing Imagination
- Large, edged cookie sheet filled with sand or dirt
- CD player and Taizé song, "Lord Jesus Christ," from the CD titled *Sing to God,* or another hymn

Week 5 : Group Meditation with Scripture
- Several votive candles, matches or lighter

PART 3   DEEPENING OUR PRAYER: THE HEART OF CHRIST

Week 1: Prayer and the Character of God
- Art material, including modeling clay or play dough
- Recorded meditative music for background
- Printout of groups from the *Companions* Web site, if choosing to be a partner group

Week 2: Dealing with Impediments to Prayer
- Handouts or newsprint with Dietrich Bonhoeffer's *Life Together* quote (page 95)

Week 3: Prayers of Petition and Intercession
- No additional materials required

Week 4: Praying As We Are
- Pictures or art that depict people in human situations for option #1
- Arrangements made for field trip (option #2)

Week 5: Psalms, the Prayer Book of the Bible
- No additional materials required

Week 6: Exploring Contemplative Prayer
- Play dough or modeling clay and art materials
- Small bell or chime, or CD or audiocassette player with meditative music selection
- Handouts of Reflection Sheet (page 119)
- Handouts or newsprint with words to the song, "Spirit of the Living God"
- *Optional*: Communion elements if doing the Lord's Supper
- Music to "Here I Am, Lord"

PART 4 RESPONDING TO OUR CALL: THE WORK OF CHRIST

Week 1: Radical Availability
- Handouts on burning bush (page 127)

Week 2: Living Reliance
- A small candle or votive for each person, matches or lighter
- A small amount of play dough or modeling clay for each person
- *Optional*: CD or audiocassette player and quiet background music
- Newsprint or cards with words from Isaiah 60:1 (pages 133)
- Words of 2 Corinthians 12:9 on newsprint (page 133)
- A small amount of olive oil and a plate

Week 3: Bearing the Fruit of the Vine
- Handouts of Solitary Reflection (pages 141–42)
- Pitcher of water, two basins, and two towels
- CD or audiocassette player with meditative music
- Hand towel or washcloth for each participant

Week 4: Gifts of the Spirit
- No additional materials required

Week 5: The Body of Christ Given for the World
- *Optional*: Communion elements

PART 5 EXPLORING SPIRITUAL GUIDANCE: THE SPIRIT OF CHRIST

Week 1: How Do I Know God's Will for My Life
- Handout of the "Holy Listening Exercise" (pages 159–60)
- Bell or chime
- Newsprint with three columns with headings (page 161)

Week 2: Spiritual Companions
- A copy of the Leader's Notes for the facilitator or clerk of the Clearness Committee (pages 167–68)

Week 3: Small Groups for Spiritual Guidance
- Newsprint with a rough, unfinished sketch of the church as a garden based on Catherine of Siena (Participant's Book, page 259; Part 5, p. 41)

- Colored pencils or colored markers
- Tacks or tape to hang drawings

Week 4: Re-Visioning Our Life As Companions in Christ
- Option 1: Handouts or newsprint with an issue of concern in your congregation
- Option 2: Handouts or newsprint with two alternative proposals (page 176)

Week 5: Re-Visioning Our Need for Guidance
- Sticky notes in two colors

CLOSING RETREAT FOR 28-WEEK COMPANIONS IN CHRIST

- Appropriate retreat site
- Handouts of a common liturgy or use one in the hymnals
- Handouts of "Solitary Reflection Questions" (page 194)
- Blank paper for writing testimonies
- Appropriate meal arrangements
- Items for worship center/table
- Newsprint and markers
- Communion elements

Introduction

*A*s a convenience for groups who want to take breaks between the parts of *Companions in Christ* or who want to sample one part at a time, we have provided the Participant's Book in two formats: one comprehensive volume for use with the 28-week experience and one in five separate volumes—one for each part of *Companions in Christ*. This Leader's Guide was written with the assumption that your group will complete the 28-week experience. In this revised Leader's Guide, when we refer to the page numbers in the Participant's Book, the one-volume paging is referred to first, while the page numbers for the five-volume set appear in parentheses (e.g., Part 1, p. 15).

Companions in Christ is designed to create a setting where you and other people in your church can respond to God's call to an ever-deepening communion and wholeness in Christ—as individuals, as members of a small group, and as part of a congregation. The resource focuses on your experience of God and your discovery of spiritual practices for sharing more fully in the life of Christ. Participants will explore the potential of Christian community as an environment of grace and mutual guidance through the Spirit. The small group will grow closer as you seek together to know and respond to God's will. And your congregation will grow when you and your companions begin to bring what you learn into all areas of church life, from classes and meetings to worship and outreach.

Companions in Christ is also designed to develop persons like you for leadership roles in guiding the spiritual life of the congregation. This resource gives you an overview of the Christian spiritual life and the practices that help people enter into the formative pattern of Christ's life; a life of prayer, study, and service. *Companions* exposes you to spiritual wisdom and guidance drawn from the full spectrum of our historic Christian heritage, including contributions from early Christian leaders and reformers as well as modern spiritual writers. More significantly, this Leader's Guide will assist you in creating a welcoming space for your group members to seek God, to share their lives in Christ, and to explore practices of opening to the Spirit's guidance. What you learn from your leadership role will assist your participation in other spiritual formation ministries within your congregation.

Before looking at the specific content and design of *Companions in Christ*, you may want to consider how this resource addresses two important questions. First, how does *Companions in Christ* help you and your group to grow spiritually? Taken separately or together, the five units enable you to immerse yourself in streams of living waters through the spiritual disciplines of prayer, scripture, study, worship, ministry, and Christian conversation. These means of grace are the common ways in which Christ meets people, renews their faith, and deepens their life together in love.

- Through *Companions*, you will explore the depths of scripture, learn to listen to God through it, and allow your life to be shaped by the Word.

- Through *Companions*, you will experience new dimensions of prayer, try fresh ways of opening to God, and learn what it means to practice the presence of God.

- Through *Companions*, you will reflect on Christ's call in your life and discover anew the gifts that God gives you for living out your personal ministry.

- Through *Companions*, you and members of your group will grow together as a Christian community and gain skills in learning how small groups in the church become settings for spiritual guidance.

Second, for whom is *Companions in Christ* designed? *Companions* is for spiritually hungry persons who seek a deeper experience of God in company with others in the Christian community. Though not an introductory course in Christianity for new Christians, *Companions* is a study for church people who want to explore afresh the basic disciplines of faith and the pathways of lifelong growth in Christ. Though *Companions* assumes a basic familiarity with the Bible that one might gain from church school, it is for persons who do not think they have all the answers, who are willing to hear scripture in new ways, and who acknowledge their need to grow in God's grace.

Companions in Christ has two primary components: (1) individual reading and daily exercises throughout the week with the Participant's Book and (2) a weekly two-hour meeting based on suggestions in this Leader's Guide. For each week, the Participant's Book has a weekly reading that introduces new material and five daily exercises to help participants reflect on their lives in light of the content of the reading. These exercises aim to help participants move from information (knowledge about) to experience (knowledge of). An important part of this process involves keeping a personal notebook or journal where participants record reflections, prayers, and questions for later review and for reference at the weekly group meeting. The daily exercise commitment is about thirty minutes. The weekly meeting will include time for reflecting on the past week's exercises, for moving deeper into learnings from the weekly readings, for having group experiences of prayer, and for considering ways to share with the congregation what has been learned or experienced.

The material in *Companions in Christ* covers a period of twenty-eight weeks divided into five parts or units, as well as an introductory or preparatory meeting and a closing retreat. The five parts are as follows:

1. *Embracing the Journey: The Way of Christ* (five weeks)—a basic exploration of spiritual formation as a journey toward holiness and wholeness, individually and in community, through the grace of God.

2. *Feeding on the Word: The Mind of Christ* (five weeks)—an introduction to several ways of meditating on and praying with scripture.

3. *Deepening Our Prayer: The Heart of Christ* (six weeks)—a guided experience of various forms and styles of prayer.

4. *Responding to Our Call: The Work of Christ* (five weeks)—a presentation of vocation or call; giving ourselves to God in radical obedience and receiving the fruits and gifts of the Holy Spirit.

5. *Exploring Spiritual Guidance: The Spirit of Christ* (five weeks)—an overview of different ways of receiving and offering spiritual guidance, from one-on-one relationships to spiritual growth groups to guidance in congregational life as a whole.

Groups may want to take a short break for a week or two between each part to allow for some unstructured reflection time or to avoid meeting near holidays. However, the parts are designed to be sequential. New members may find it difficult to enter the process once the group has established trust and identity.

The Companions in Christ Network

An additional dimension of *Companions in Christ* is the Network. While you and your group are experiencing *Companions*, groups in other congregations will also be meeting. The Network provides opportunities for you to share your experiences with one another and to link in a variety of meaningful ways. As you move through the resource, upon occasion you will be invited to pray for another group, send greetings or encouragement, or receive support for your group. Connecting in these ways will enrich your group's experience and the experience of those to whom you reach out.

The Network also provides a place for sharing conversation and information. The *Companions* Web site, www.companionsinchrist.org, includes a discussion room where you can offer insights, voice questions, and respond to others in an ongoing process of shared learning. The site provides a list of other *Companions* groups and their geographical locations so you can make connections as you feel led. Locations and dates for Leader Orientations (basic one-day trainings) and the Leader Trainings (advanced three-day trainings) are posted here; you will also find supplemental resource suggestions.

The *Companions* Network is a versatile and dynamic component of the larger *Companions* resource. A Network toll free number 1-800-972-0433 is staffed during regular business hours to take your order.

The Role of the Small-Group Leader

Leading a group for spiritual formation differs in many ways from teaching a class. The most obvious difference comes in your basic goal as group leader. In a class, you have particular information (facts, theories, ways of doing things) that you want to convey. You can gauge your success at the end of the class if participants demonstrate some grasp of the information. In a group for spiritual formation, your goal is to enable spiritual growth in each participant. You work in partnership with the Holy Spirit, who alone can bring about transformation of the human heart. Here gaining wisdom is more important than gaining knowledge, and growing in holiness is more important than gaining either knowledge or wisdom. Success, if it has any meaning in this context, will be evident over months and even years in the changed lives of group members.

Classes tend to be task-oriented. Groups for spiritual formation tend to be more process-oriented. Even though group members will have done common preparation in reading and daily exercises, group discussions may move in directions you do not expect. You will need to be open to the movement of the Holy Spirit and vigilant in discerning the difference between following the Spirit's lead and going off on a tangent. Such discernment requires careful, prayerful listening. Listening will be much more important than talking in your role as group leader.

Finally, classes have as their primary focus some set of objective data. It could be a Bible passage, information from a book, or interpretations of current events. In a group for spiritual formation, however, the primary focus is on the personal faith experience of each group member. Each person is seeking to understand and be open to the grace and revelation of God. Even when group members have read and reflected on a scripture passage, the basis for group discussion is not "What did the author intend to say to readers of that time?" but "How does this passage connect to my life or illuminate my experience?" Discussion will be a sharing of experience, not a debate over ideas. You will model this type of personal sharing with your group because of your involvement in all parts of the group meeting. The type of leadership needed differs from that of a traditional teacher of a church school class or small-group facilitator. As leader, you will read the material and complete the daily exercises along with other members and bring your responses to share with the group. You lead by offering your honest reflections and by trying to enable the group members to listen carefully to one another and to the Spirit in your midst.

Leading a group for spiritual formation requires particular qualities. Foremost among these are patience and trust. You will need patience to let things happen as they happen. Spiritual formation is a lifelong process. It may be difficult to identify any great leaps forward during the several months the group will spend on *Companions in Christ*. It may even take a while for group members to adjust to the purpose and style of a formational group process. As a group leader, you need to resolve that when you ask a question, you do not have a "right answer" in mind; you want participants to talk about their own experience. Setting an example of sharing your experience rather than proclaiming abstract truths or talking about the experiences of other well-known Christians will move this shift along. You trust that the Holy Spirit will indeed help group members to see or hear what they really need. You may offer what you consider a great insight to which no one responds. If the group needs that insight, the Spirit will bring it around again at a more opportune time. Susan Muto, a modern writer on spiritual formation, often says that we need to "make space for the pace of grace." There are no shortcuts to spiritual growth. Be patient and trust the Spirit.

Listening is another critical quality for a leader of a spiritual formation group. This does not mean simply listening for people to say what you hope they will say, so you can jump in and reinforce them. You need to listen for what is actually going on. What is actually happening in participants' minds and hearts may be quite different from what you expect after reading the material and doing the weekly exercises yourself. While you listen, you might want to jot down brief notes about themes that emerge in the discussion. Does a particular type of experience seem to be at the center of the sharing? Is a particular direction or common understanding emerging—a hint of God's will or a shared sense of what was especially helpful to several group members? Is there some action that group members need to take together or individually in order to move forward or respond to an emerging sense of call? What do you hear again and again?

A group leader also needs to be accepting. Accept that group members may have had spiritual experiences quite different from yours. Accept that people often see common experiences in different ways. Some may be struck by something that did not impress you at all, while others may be left cold by things that really excite or move you. As you model acceptance, you will help foster acceptance of one another's differences within the group. Beyond accepting differences, you will need to accept lack of closure. Group meetings will rarely tie up all the loose ends in a neat package. Burning questions will be left hanging. If important, they will surface again (which brings us back to patience and trust). Also be prepared to accept people's emotions along with their thoughts and experiences. Tears, fears, joy, and anger are to be received as legitimate responses along this journey. One important expression of acceptance is permission-giving. Permit people to grow and share at their own pace. Let group members know in your first meeting that while you want to encourage full participation in every part of the process, they are free to "opt out" of anything that makes them feel truly uncomfortable. No one will be forced to share or pray without consent. "Where the Spirit of the Lord is, there is freedom" (2 Cor. 3:17).

It is particularly important to avoid three common tendencies:

1. *Fixing.* When someone presents a specific problem, it will be tempting to want to find a solution and "fix" the problem. Problem solving generally makes us feel better. Perhaps it makes us feel wise or powerful or it helps to break the tension, but it will not help the other to grow. Moreover, we might prescribe the wrong fix! It is far better, if you have had a similar problem, to speak about your own experience and what worked for you. If you have not had direct experience, perhaps someone else in the group has.

2. *Proselytizing.* You know what has brought you closer to God. Naturally you would like everyone to try it. You can offer your own experience to the group, but it is dangerous spiritually to try to convince everyone to follow your path. Here is where your knowledge and wisdom come into play. Teresa of Avila said that if she had to choose between

a holy spiritual director and a learned one, she would pick the learned one. The saint might be able to talk only about his or her own spiritual path. The learned one might at least recognize another person's experience from having read about such experiences. It is far more useful to be able to clarify and celebrate someone else's experience than to urge others to try to follow your way.

3. *Controlling.* Many of us are accustomed to filling in silence with some comment. It may be tempting to see ourselves as experts with an appropriate response to whatever anyone says; that is, we tend to dominate and control the conversation. Here, again, patience and listening are essential. Do not be afraid of silence. Your capacity to be comfortable with silence allows you to be a "nonanxious presence" in the group. If you really cannot bear a long silence, it is better to break it with an invitation for someone (maybe someone who has been quiet so far) to share a thought, feeling, or question than with some comment of your own.

If this style of leadership seems challenging or unfamiliar to you, please seriously consider attending a leader training event for *Companions in Christ.* While leadership training is not required for this resource, it is highly recommended and strongly encouraged.

Expectations for the "Sharing Insights" Section of Each Meeting

This section offers a basic process for the first hour of your group session, the parts titled "Opening" and "Sharing Insights" in the lesson plans. The pattern that you follow during this time can be used for any small group for spiritual growth. In other groups, you could substitute readings from a spiritual classic or meditation on selected passages of scripture for the readings and exercises in *Companions in Christ.*

The first step in the group session is prayer and a time of quiet centering. Invoking the Holy Spirit's guiding presence is especially important in the "Opening," or gathering portion of the weekly group meeting (see "A General Outline of Each Group Meeting," pages 21–24).

Most of the "Sharing Insights" part of the group session will focus on individual members talking about their experiences with the daily exercises. Encourage members to bring their journals to refresh their memories of the week's exercises. You, as leader, will generally want to model by beginning with your own sharing, which sets the tone for the rest of the group. Make your sharing brief (two to three minutes), allowing ample time for others to share. Above all, let it be specific, dealing with your response to one of the exercises. You need not announce a general topic. The rest of the group will have read the material and done the exercises. If your sharing is general or abstract, other participants will be less likely to share personal experiences. On occasion, this guide will offer suggestions for your sharing. Follow them only if they reflect your own response to the material. Your initial sharing in this part of the group meeting is one of your most important roles as the leader. Consider carefully each week what you would like to share, remaining mindful of how your sharing helps establish trust in the group as well as the serious intent of this part of the meeting.

During the "Sharing Insights" time, your main job is to listen. Listen primarily for themes—similar experiences that suggest a general truth about the spiritual life, common responses to the readings that might indicate a word God wants the group to hear, or recurring experiences that might offer practical help to other group members as they try to hear and respond to God's call. Take notes so you can lift up these themes as the "Sharing Insights" time comes to an end. You will also invite the other group members to share any themes or patterns they may have identified from the discussion. You can listen for key differences in participants' experiences and affirm the variety of ways God speaks to and guides each one of us. You need to be alert to the temptation of participants to "fix" problems, control conversation, or proselytize. Gently remind them to share their *own* experiences or reactions. The same guidance applies if a participant mentions someone else as an example, whether in the group or outside it. Nothing can destroy group trust more quickly than exposing confidences.

By establishing up front some ground rules for group sharing, you may avoid problems. In the Preparatory Meeting, you will explain the various components of each week's meeting. It would be good to discuss the nature of this sharing time and establish some basic ground rules for the group. Here are some suggestions:

• Speak only for yourself about beliefs, feelings, and responses.

• Respect and receive what others offer, even if you disagree.

• Listening is more important than talking. Avoid cross-talk, interrupting, speaking for others, or trying to "fix" another person's problems.

• Honor the different ways God works in individuals.

• Do not be afraid of silence. Use it to listen to the Spirit in your midst.

• Maintain confidentiality. What is shared in the group stays in the group.

- Recognize that all group members have permission to share only what and when they are ready to share.

You may want to add to this list before you share it with the group.

A few minutes before the scheduled end of the group sharing session, state aloud any themes you have noted during the discussion: a summary report on what you have actually heard, not a chance to "get in the last word" on various topics of discussion. It can be fairly brief: "I noticed that several of us were particularly drawn to the parable of the banquet in Exercise 4 this week. I wonder if God is trying to call our attention to something here—maybe our church's selectivity in inviting outsiders." Note that this is a time not for moving the discussion to a more abstract level but for summarizing and tying together some themes of the discussion, which has already taken place.

Finally, you may want to close this part of the group session with prayer. You may pray for the deepening of particular insights, for the ability to follow through on the themes or guidance you have heard, or for God's leading on questions that have been left open. You may feel a need to pray for particular situations that have been mentioned. And you may want to invite all group members who are willing to offer simple sentence prayers of their own.

A General Outline of Each Group Meeting

The weekly group meetings will typically follow the outline explained below. Within the outline are two overall movements: one primarily emphasizes sharing insights and learning from the week's reading and daily exercises; the other primarily develops a deeper understanding of spiritual disciplines or practices. The first movement generally will be a group discussion as described in the preceding section. Sometimes, particularly in the beginning, a more structured approach will be necessary. The second part of the meeting, called "Deeper Explorations," may expand on ideas contained in the week's reading, offer practice in spiritual exercises being taught in the reading, or give group members a chance to reflect on the implications of what they are learning for their own journeys and for the church. It may include a brief look forward if special preparation is needed for the coming week.

Both movements are intended as times of formation. In the first, the focus is on the group members' responses to the weekly reading and exercises. The second movement focuses on expanding and deepening the content of the reading.

Consider carefully the setting for your group meetings. An adaptable space is important for group process. Most often, the best arrangement is a circle of comfortable chairs or sofas. On occasion participants might want a table for writing. Since the group will sometimes break into pairs or triads, space to separate is also important. The space for meeting will need to be relatively quiet and peaceful.

It helps to create a worship focus for the group, at least for opening and closing times. This might be as simple as a candle on a small table in the center of the circle. It could be more elaborate, with pictures, sculpture, flowers, shells, or cloths changing from week to week. Maybe someone in the group would enjoy setting up the worship center as a special project. Or you might want to rotate the responsibility for creating a worship focus. Either way, you might want to keep a few items handy as backups. Remember, the purpose is to help participants center on God's presence with them; therefore, make the worship focus central to the circle or part of the circle.

OPENING (10 MINUTES)

This brief time of worship will give group members a chance to quiet down and prepare for the group session to follow. Each group will eventually discover what works best for its members. The Leader's Guide offers some specific suggestions, but you can develop your own pattern of prayer and centering, if you desire. Possibilities for this opening worship include 1) singing a hymn together, whether one that is sung at the beginning of every meeting or one that is specially selected each week; 2) silence; 3) lighting a candle; 4) scripture reading; 5) individual prayer, planned or extemporaneous; or 6) group prayer using a written or memorized prayer. Some hymns or songs that might be suitable for this beginning time are "Surely the Presence of the Lord"; "Sweet, Sweet Spirit"; "Spirit Song"; "Sanctuary"; "Lord, Be Glorified"; "Into My Heart"; and "Ubi Caritas."

SHARING INSIGHTS (45 MINUTES)

The content for this part of the meeting comes from reading the material for the week and working through the five daily exercises that group members have completed since the last meeting. If members fail to read the material or skip the daily exercises, they will be left out. If too many come unprepared, the group process simply will not work. Group discussion generally will follow the model given above under "Expectations for the 'Sharing Insights' Section of Each Meeting." Since the "Opening" has provided prayer and centering time, this section would begin with sharing from you as the group leader, continue with group discussion, and end with whatever summarizing you feel is helpful, followed by a brief prayer. You will need to keep an eye on the time in order to bring the discussion to a close and have time for summary and prayer. Occasionally this time will need a different structure such as for personal introductions and spiritual autobiographies.

BREAK (10 MINUTES)

Group break time serves several important purposes physically, mentally, and relationally. It also gives some time for snacking if you arrange for someone to provide food. Do not neglect or squeeze out adequate break time, and be sure to take a break yourself as leader.

DEEPER EXPLORATIONS (45 MINUTES)

This part of the group meeting builds on material in the weekly reading and daily exercises. The content for this time takes three primary forms. It may expand on the reading through discussion of related materials. It may apply the reading through exercises, relating its content to the lives of individual members, to the life of the group as a whole, or to the church. Finally, it may offer further practice in the disciplines explored in the exercises, either by going through a similar exercise in the group or by presenting alternative ways of practicing these disciplines. This segment of the meeting is very important. It is like the experiential part of a spiritual retreat in miniature and requires your thoughtful preparation as the leader if you are to guide the process comfortably. Please review the leader material early in the week prior to the meeting so that you have time to think through the process and complete any preparation.

CLOSING (10 MINUTES)

As it began, the group meeting ends with a time of worship. First, though, you may need to attend to practical matters of meeting place or provision of refreshments if these vary from week to week. You may also draw names for prayer partners for the coming week and ask for prayer requests.

The Leader's Guide includes suggestions for the "Closing." If you choose to develop your own plans, consider the following ideas: the time of closing worship may include intercessions for special requests, prayers that flow from the content of the group's meeting, and any other prayers group members feel led to offer. You may want to finish with the Lord's Prayer to place these specific prayers in the context of the universal prayer of Christ's church.

You may want to conclude the entire meeting with a hymn or song. Here are some appropriate ones: "Blest Be the Tie That Binds," "Sent Forth by God's Blessing," "Shalom to You," "Lord, Dismiss Us with Thy Blessing," or "God Be with You till We Meet Again."

Concluding Matters

Because churches of various Christian traditions will be using this resource, you may need to adapt some of the worship experiences or experiences related to baptism and the Lord's Supper to suit your own tradition. The Leader's Guide suggests songs for each weekly meeting, but they are only suggestions. Each group will have access to different hymnals and songbooks and will have its own preference in musical style. The Leader's Guide also includes a list of supplemental music information and ordering sources on pages 243–44. If you or some persons in your group have musical ability, you might choose to use these additional resources. The Participant's Book includes a song written specifically for *Companions in Christ*, called "Companion Song." It includes annotations both for piano and guitar accompaniment. The music is easy to learn, and the song could serve as a theme song for your group. We encourage you to try it in your Preparatory Meeting and to use it several times during your early meetings. If the group likes it, the participants will naturally ask to sing it as you move through your time together.

The purpose of *Companions in Christ* is to equip persons of faith with both personal and corporate spiritual life practices that will continue long beyond the time frame of this particular resource. Participants may continue certain disciplines on their own or carry some practices into congregational life. Others may desire the continuation of a small group. You will likely discover, as you guide your group through this journey, that certain topics generate interest and energy for further exploration. Some group members may wish that certain readings or weekly meetings could go into more depth than they do. When the group expresses strong desire to continue with a particular topic or practice, take special note of it. A number of possibilities exist for small-group study and practice beyond this resource. Some suggested resources are listed in the Participant's Book. Your group will make decisions about future directions toward the end of this experience, particularly during the closing retreat.

Our prayer for you as a leader is that the weeks ahead will lead you and your group deeper into the heart and mind, the work and spirit, the very life of Jesus Christ. May your companionship with Christ and with one another be richly blessed!

Preparatory Meeting

*T*he Leader's Guide of *Companions in Christ* addresses most of the material concerning each group meeting directly to you as the leader. Occasionally the Leader's Guide also offers suggested words for you to speak to the group as a way of introducing various sections. Where this occurs, the words are printed in a light bold typeface (such as the first item under "Set the context"). Be assured that these words are only suggestions. Always feel free to express the same idea in your own words or adapt it as you deem necessary.

Plan this Preparatory Meeting at the beginning of the 28-week experience. Or, if your group decides to take lengthy breaks between parts, plan to have the meeting again at the beginning of Parts 2–5.

PREPARATION

Prepare yourself spiritually. Review the material in the introduction to the Participant's Book(s), as well as the information in the introduction to the Leader's Guide. Look over the Contents page in the Participant's Book(s) so you can answer questions that may arise. Pray for each group member and for the beginning of your journey together as companions in Christ. Also pray that God might guide you in your role of leader so that your small group may begin this time together with openness and genuine expectation.

Prepare any materials or equipment. Arrange for hymnals or songbooks and for accompaniment if possible. Select the hymns or songs that you want to use for the "Opening" and "Closing." Also select the scripture text for your opening worship (see suggestions below). Set up chairs in a circle with a center table and candle. Make sure you have a copy of the Participant's Book for each person. Have paper and pencil for each participant for the journaling exercise. Provide nametags and markers if your group members don't know one another well.

Review the intent of this meeting: that participants will have a clear understanding of the purpose of *Companions in Christ*, that they have an opportunity to express their questions as well as their hopes and dreams for this journey, and that they see clearly the expectations that are a part of their decision to participate in the group.

OPENING (10 MINUTES)

Welcome all participants by name as they enter.

Set the context.

- This meeting is in preparation for a new venture we are going to undertake together called *Companions in Christ*. It is a small-group resource in spiritual formation that will lead us through a journey of experiential learning and close with a retreat.

- We will want to talk through a number of things in this meeting; but before we do, it will be good to take a brief time to worship together, bringing ourselves and this venture before God in prayer.

Join together in worship.

- Light a candle as a symbol of the presence of Christ's light in our midst and say, **Whenever we gather, we are together in the active presence of Jesus Christ.**

- Read a passage of scripture that speaks to the theme of preparation, such as Isaiah 40:3-5 or Mark 1:1-3.

- How do we "prepare the way of the Lord"? Take a few moments of quiet to ponder what it might mean to prepare our hearts for this experience together. What do we need to do inwardly or outwardly? What do we need to let go of or make room for in order to let God make of this time what God wants it to be—for us and through us for our congregation?

- Offer a word of prayer for openness of mind and heart to the guiding grace of the Holy Spirit and for God's blessing on each person and on the whole process.

- Sing a song or hymn such as "Prepare Ye the Way of the Lord" (from *Godspell*); "Jesus, United by Thy Grace"; or any song of praise.

INTRODUCTIONS AND SHARING OF EXPECTATIONS (45 MINUTES)

Use as much time as needed for introductions, even if group members are sure they know one another already. Start by inviting members to pair up with the person each knows least well to share some basic information about name, family, work in the world, and work in the church. Pair members can then introduce each other to the rest of the group. Next, invite each person to talk about what brought him or her to be part of this group at this time. If some answer, "So-and-so asked me," follow up by asking why they said yes. Continue, as time permits, with other questions such as:

- **What do you hope will happen to you through being part of this group?**

- **What image does the phrase *spiritual formation* call to your mind?**

BREAK (10 MINUTES)

PRESENTATION OF RESOURCES AND GROUP PROCESS (45 MINUTES)

Use this time to talk about the group process and about expectations of individual group members. If you have not yet done so, hand out the Participant's Books. Be familiar with the material in the introductions to the Participant's Book and to the Leader's Guide. Go over this content with group members so that each person understands the process of the reading, daily exercises, and journaling, as well as the outline for each group meeting. Here are some items you will want to mention:

Basic flow of the week. Ask each participant to read the material for the week on Day 1 (the day after the group meeting) and work through the five exercises over Days 2–6. Encourage participants' faithfulness to the process, and suggest that they read over their notebooks/journals for the week after doing the fifth exercise. The group meeting is Day 7.

Basic flow of a group meeting. Explain the various components: "Opening," "Sharing Insights," "Deeper Explorations," and "Closing." Summarize for the group the explanatory material found on pages 22–24 of the introduction to the Leader's Guide.

More detailed explanation of the "Sharing Insights" section of the group meeting. Summarize material from pages 19–21 in the Leader's Guide. Emphasize the importance of each member's commitment to daily exercises for the group process to work. Because some group members will have no experience with this type of group process and interaction, you will need to help them feel comfortable with it and to explain the basic simplicity of the sharing with one another. Remind them that one way we listen to God is to put our experience into words. The very process of articulation often brings clarity and new perspective. Therefore the group becomes a space for deep listening and trusting in God's guiding presence.

Ground rules for discussion. Be prepared to present some ground rules such as the ones listed on pages 20–21 in this book, and allow the members to suggest others.

Explanation of journaling. Use the material in the introduction to the Participant's Book(s). The leader can help participants understand the importance to this resource of recording reflections in a journal, a personal notebook, or the blank pages at the end of the Participant's Books. Please assure them that the writing can be as informal and unstructured as they want. Each person will keep whatever notes are most helpful to him or her, and the journal becomes the personal record of the spiritual-growth journey that this resource is designed to encourage. You might want to give those gathered a chance to try out a brief exercise in journaling right now. Explain that you would like to give them a flavor of what it is like to journal without regard to complete sentences, accurate punctuation, or correct spelling. Invite them to spend just a few minutes jotting down spontaneously any thoughts, insights, questions, or words that seem important based on the time you have spent together in this gathering so far. Allow three or four minutes for this exercise, and then ask how it felt to do this. Encourage people to experiment and find a style of journaling that feels free, not burdensome.

Materials for each meeting. Ask members to bring a Bible, the Participant's Book, and their journals to each meeting. Because they will be using the Bible as a part of the daily exercises, you may want to encourage persons to use a contemporary translation that contains study aids. (See the list of suggested study Bibles on page 233 of this Leader's Guide.)

CLOSING (10 MINUTES)

Remind everyone of the first assignment for the upcoming week in preparation for the next group meeting. Be sure all participants know the location and time of the next meeting and any special responsibilities (such as providing snacks or helping to arrange the worship table).

Invite a time of quiet reflection. **What are your hopes for the time ahead of us as companions in Christ? What are your anxieties about this time? Commit both your hopes and your fears to God in silent prayer now.**

Offer a brief word of prayer, asking that we all might be able to release our hopes and concerns into God's good and gracious hands. End with thanksgiving for each person and for God's wonderful purposes in bringing this group together.

Introduce the "Companion Song" in the back of the Participant's Book(s). Teach it or ask a musical member of your group to do so.

Say or sing a benediction such as "Shalom My Friends" or "Ubi Caritas."

Part 1

Embracing the Journey: The Way of Christ

Introductory Leader's Notes for Part 1

*P*art 1 presents the Christian life as a lifelong journey of transformation in Christ, traveled in faithful companionship with one another. It is your privilege as group leader to facilitate a learning process by which members of your group rediscover their spiritual identities, God's presence in their life journeys, and their companionship together in Christ.

Before you begin preparing for Week 1, take a few minutes to survey the whole of Part 1 in the Participant's Book and Leader's Guide. Familiarize yourself with the intent of the five weekly readings and the flow of the five weekly meetings. Scan the section called "Preparation" on the first page of all five weeks in Part 1 of the Leader's Guide. Also check the "Needs at a Glance" list for Part 1 on page 8 of this revised Leader's Guide. This will ensure that you know ahead of time the supplies you need to gather to facilitate the group work, worship, and singing. Be sure to make copies of all the necessary handouts.

Anticipate the possible need for additional time to complete Week 4's session, especially if you have more than eight persons in your group including yourself. Prior to publication, the *Companions in Christ* resources were tested in a number of churches. These test groups found the sharing of spiritual journeys in Week 4 to be a pivotal experience that required adequate time for each person. This session should not be abbreviated or rushed. The test groups successfully dealt with the need for more time by extending the meeting time or arranging a special meeting for the sole purpose of completing the faith stories. The test groups that completed the sharing of spiritual journeys by squeezing it into the next week's meeting found that they compromised Week 5. The theme in Week 5 of living as a covenant community challenges many people, and the allotted time for sharing insights and for deeper exploration is necessary. Also, some groups chose to extend Week 5 in order to bring closure to the whole unit with a brief worship service of Holy Communion.

Be deliberate about moving the group from the "Sharing Insights" to the "Deeper Explorations" segments in a timely way, following a break. The test groups found that the time of "Sharing Insights" was sometimes so meaningful that people had difficulty shifting into the second half of the meeting. Be aware that it is also a natural temptation for people to remain in a more familiar discussion mode, rather than to venture into new experiential learning processes. During the break, people will naturally want to continue their conversations. Refreshments during the break may prolong the transition and compromise the time available for "Deeper Explorations."

Prepare for worship as carefully as you prepare for "Sharing Insights" and "Deeper Explorations." Consider whether you want to create a separate adjacent worship space for the "Opening" and "Closing." Adapt the suggestions for opening each meeting to suit the temperaments and traditions of your group as well as the theme of the session. Review the "Supplemental Music Resources" section at the back of this guide for additional song possibilities and decide in which meetings you would like to use "Companion Song" again for Openings or Closings.

Closings, though usually brief, are integral to the session and also require careful preparation. The test groups confirmed the importance of bringing closure to sessions with worship. In Week 2, for example, the "Closing" is the formative event that turns a theological concept into a spiritual experience.

May God be with you as you guide the group members toward becoming companions in Christ.

The Christian Life As Journey

PREPARATION

Prepare yourself spiritually. Review the material in the introduction, especially the sections titled "The Role of the Small-Group Leader" and "Expectations for the 'Sharing Insights' Section of Each Meeting." Read the material for Week 1, "The Christian Life as Journey," in the Participant's Book, do all the exercises, and keep a journal along with other participants. Pray for each participant and for your ability to be present to God in and through the group meeting.

Prepare any materials or equipment. Arrange for hymnals or songbooks and for accompaniment if possible. Select the hymns or songs you want to use for the "Opening" and "Closing." Set up chairs in a circle with a center table and candle. Make sure that you have sufficient copies of the handout exercise on Ephesians 4 (page 37).

Review the intent of this meeting: that participants deepen their understanding of their faith life as a spiritual journey and the goal of the journey as maturity in Christ.

OPENING (10 MINUTES)

Welcome all participants by name as they enter.

Set the context.

- **This meeting is the first session of five that is designed to help us discover the nature of our Christian lives as journeys toward maturity in Christ. This part of *Companions* will allow us to share our daily progress, reflect on learnings, deal with difficulties, and help one another to overcome obstacles.**

- Even though you spent some time in introductions during the preparatory meeting, take a few minutes to get better acquainted with one another. If group members do not know one another well, invite all participants to say their names again and one thing few people know about them. Set the example by sharing briefly something fun or unusual about yourself that is not deeply intimate. For example, "My name is _____, and one thing most people don't know about me is that when I was young I dreamed of being a concert pianist."

Join together in worship.

- **We light the candle as a way of remembering God's presence with us as we set out on our journey as companions in Christ. Last week we shared a little about why each of us is here. Listen now to these words from Psalm 27:1, 4:**

> The LORD is my light and my salvation;
>   whom shall I fear?
> The LORD is the stronghold of my life;
>   of whom shall I be afraid? . . .
> One thing I asked of the LORD,
>   that will I seek after:
> to live in the house of the LORD
>   all the days of my life,
> to behold the beauty of the LORD,
>   and to inquire in his temple.

- **In silence take a moment to ponder, What is the one thing you ask of the Lord, the one thing you seek?**

- Sing a song together such as "When You Seek Me"; "Come, My Way, My Truth, My Life"; "On This Day"; "Kum Ba Yah"; "All the Way My Savior Leads Me"; "Guide Me, O Thou Great Jehovah."

- Offer a brief opening prayer.

SHARING INSIGHTS (45 MINUTES)

Look briefly at this week's reading (10 minutes).

- Summarize the three basic ideas here: 1) that the Christian life is a journey; 2) that it is characterized by three movements: being oriented, becoming disoriented, and being surprisingly reoriented; and 3) that the journey leads toward maturity in Christ.

- Invite participants to share any insights or questions from the reading they would especially like to highlight before sharing experiences with the daily exercises. Ask them to discuss any places where they found themselves saying, "Yes!" or "No" or "What?" Keep the dialogue brief and focused on the reading.

Introduce sharing in small groups (5 minutes).

- If you did not discuss ground rules for the group sharing when you gathered for your preparatory meeting, please set aside some time for the group to explore this subject. Please reread the bulleted list on pages 20–21 as background for this discussion. It is most important that groups begin with some shared understandings about confidentiality and a process for sharing around the daily exercises.

- Form two or three subgroups (three to four persons in each; leader will join also). Explain that the group sharing will occur in subgroups for the first two meetings, but then the larger group will participate together for this part of the meeting.

- This week's exercises invited exploration of our lives as spiritual journeys. Exercises 1 through 4 build toward Exercise 5. Begin your sharing with Exercise 5 and move to others as time allows.

- Encourage participants to listen for God in each person's reflections and stories.

- As leader, model sharing by offering your response to Exercise 5 first, referring to the biblical text and exercise (take two to three minutes, then join a group to listen).

Share in small groups (25 minutes).

Invite participants to begin small-group sharing with a few minutes of quiet reflecting and review of their journals.

Gather together (5 minutes).

Invite everyone to pause and note briefly any patterns of journey and awareness of God's presence that were shared.

BREAK (10 MINUTES)

Deeper Explorations (45 minutes)

Introduce the theme—exploring the meaning of spiritual growth and our own call to mature in Christ (5 minutes).

- The weekly reading reminds us that our spiritual journeys have a common direction and destination: maturing in Christ.

- Ask two persons to read aloud Colossians 1:28-29 and 1 John 3:2.

- Note that the authors of Part 1 write, "We have not arrived, but are moving toward . . . the fulfillment of our potential as children of God."

Exercise with Ephesians 4 (30 minutes).

One of the New Testament's finest portrayals of the nature of spiritual growth and maturity is found in the fourth chapter of Ephesians. We are going to observe a quiet time now as each of us reads Ephesians 4 and listens to God's call in the abundant images of maturing in Christ. (Use the handout exercise on page 37.)

Gather together (10 minutes).

- Ask people to sit together in pairs from their subgroup. If the subgroup was a triad, remain as three.

- Invite them to share briefly, as they are comfortable, their reflections on the maturity that beckons them and the grace for which they would ask one another to pray.

- Invite them to enter a minute or so of silent prayer for one another (pairs/triads may join hands if they like).

Closing (10 minutes)

Remind everyone of assignments for the coming week, next week's meeting place and time, and any other necessary announcements.

Invite the group to pause and absorb this time as companions in Christ. Where did they sense God's presence? When did the Spirit catch their attention? What do they find themselves longing for?

Spend some time praying together.

Say or sing a benediction, such as "Shalom to You," "Ubi Caritas," or "Companion Song."

Exercise on Ephesians 4

Solitary reflection, journaling, and prayer.

• Read Ephesians 4 slowly and prayerfully, allowing God to address you.

• Note in your journal phrases that speak of the kind of maturing for which you long. Write in your own words what those phrases mean for you.

• Reread verses 22-24, listening to what God is saying to you.

• Draw a line down the middle of a page in your journal. On the left side, name one to three aspects of your old self that you want to find the strength to "put away." On the right side, name one to three aspects of your "new self, created according to the likeness of God" that you hope to "put on."

• Share with God your desire to grow, and ask for the grace to move toward your goal.

Part 1, Week 2
The Nature of the Christian Spiritual Life

PREPARATION

Prepare yourself spiritually. Review the material in the introduction of the Leader's Guide as a reminder of the role of leadership and the formational process of the small-group sharing. Read the material for Week 2 in the Participant's Book, do all the exercises, and keep your journal. Review the Leader's Notes on scripture (page 44) for this session. Pray for each participant and for your presence to the Spirit as group leader.

Prepare any materials or equipment. Bring a bowl and a pitcher of water. Set chairs in a circle with a center table and candle. Have adequate hymnals/songbooks; select songs for the "Opening" and "Closing." Have adequate copies of the "Solitary Reflection Exercise" on Mark 1:9-11 (page 45).

Review the intent of this meeting: that participants grow in their understanding of God's grace and awareness of their identity in God.

OPENING (10 MINUTES)

Welcome all participants personally as they enter.

Set the context.

This meeting is our second session in which we are exploring the Christian spiritual life. Last week we looked at our experience of spiritual growth as a journey. This week we want to explore the grace by which we grow in God.

Join together in worship.

- **For our opening prayer, listen to Psalm 92:1-4.** (Read it slowly.)

   It is good to give thanks to the LORD,
      to sing praises to your name, O Most High;

> to declare your steadfast love in the morning,
>> and your faithfulness by night,
> to the music of the lute and the harp,
>> to the melody of the lyre.
> For you, O LORD, have made me glad by your work;
>> at the works of your hands I sing for joy.

- **During this week as you engaged in the reading and exercises, where were you especially glad? Where did you "sing for joy"?** Invite silent reflection. Encourage participants to turn to one person and share.

- Celebrate in song God's "steadfast love in the morning and faithfulness by night" such as "Blessed Assurance," "Great Is Thy Faithfulness," or "Grace Greater Than Our Sin."

- Offer a prayer of thanks, and ask for guidance.

SHARING INSIGHTS (45 MINUTES)

Look briefly at this week's reading (10 minutes).

Ask persons to look over the reading and identify the portion that spoke most clearly to them about grace. Bring out the central idea that spiritual growth is not possible apart from God's grace and a deepening trust in God's tremendous goodwill toward us. Keep the dialogue focused on the reading.

Introduce sharing in small groups (5 minutes).

- Form two or three smaller groups (three to four persons each) for sharing.

- **This week's exercises were an invitation to enter into Ephesians and the message of God's transforming grace. Now we have an opportunity to share whatever spoke to us most deeply while reading Ephesians and working through the exercises.**

- Encourage participants to practice listening for God in each person's reflections and story.

- As leader, set the tone by offering your response first, referring to the biblical text and the exercises (two to three minutes).

Share in small groups (30 minutes).

Invite participants to look briefly over their journals before sharing what spoke to them most deeply through Ephesians and the daily exercises. Five minutes before the end of sharing time, ask groups to pause for a moment of reflection: **What are you hearing and seeing as you listen to one another?**

BREAK (10 MINUTES)

DEEPER EXPLORATIONS (45 MINUTES)

Introduce the theme—reflecting on the reality of grace as the ground of our spiritual identity (20 minutes).

- In Ephesians 3:17, the writer prays that we will be "rooted and grounded in love." This is an image of where we hope to go but also of where we come from! The reality of God's grace is deeper than our awareness or experience. It is like rich soil to plants, the ground in which we are rooted and from which our lives bear fruit. This is what we celebrate in baptism.

- Invite the group members to listen quietly and respond in their journals to what they hear as you read each of the following. Leave some silence between each reading.

    1. Genesis 1:27-28

    2. Isaiah 43:1-7

    3. Henri J. M. Nouwen on "Our First Love"

        Listen to what God is saying to us:
        You are my child.
        You are written in the palms of my hand.
        You are hidden in the shadow of my hand.
        I have molded you in the secret of the earth.
        I have knitted you together in your mother's womb.
        You belong to me.
        I am yours. You are mine.
        I have called you from eternity and you are the one who is held safe and embraced
            in love from eternity to eternity.
        You belong to me. And I am holding you safe and I want you to know that what-
            ever happens to you, I am always there. I was always there; I am always there; I
            always will be there and hold you in my embrace.

> You are mine. You are my child. You belong to my home. You belong to my intimate life and I will never let you go. I will be faithful to you.
>
> The spiritual life starts at the place where you can hear God's voice. Where somehow you can claim that long before your father, your mother, your brother, your sister, your school, your church touched you, loved you, and wounded you— long before that, you were held safe in an eternal embrace. You were seen with eyes of perfect love long before you entered into the dark valley of life. . . . The spiritual life starts at the moment that you can go beyond all of the wounds and claim that there was a love that was perfect and unlimited, long before that perfect love became reflected in the imperfect and limited, conditional love of people. The spiritual life starts where you dare to claim the first love—Love one another because I have loved you first. (See 1 John 4:19)[1]

- Give all participants a chance to share what they heard with one other person.

- Gather what people have heard in short words or phrases written on newsprint.

Begin a time of solitary reflection on Mark 1:9-11 (25 minutes). Use the handout on page 45.

Closing (10 minutes)

Regather. Remind participants that they are blessed as individuals and that we as church are a community of blessing and grace.

Read a story by Janet Wolf titled "Chosen for . . . "

> In a world that pronounces so many of us "not good enough," what might it mean to believe that we really are chosen, precious, and beloved? In a new members' class we talked about baptism: this holy moment when we are named by God's grace with such power it won't come undone.
>
> Fayette was there—a woman living on the streets, struggling with mental illness and lupus. She loved the part about baptism and would ask over and over, "And when I'm baptized, I am . . . ?" We soon learned to respond, "Beloved, precious child of God and beautiful to behold." "Oh, yes!" she'd say, and then we could go back to our discussion.
>
> The big day came. Fayette went under, came up spluttering, and cried, "And now I am . . . ?" And we all sang, "Beloved, precious child of God and beautiful to behold." "Oh, yes!" she shouted as she danced all around the fellowship hall.

Two months later I got a call. Fayette had been beaten and raped and was at the county hospital. So I went. I could see her from a distance, pacing back and forth. When I got to the door, I heard, "I am beloved . . ." She turned, saw me, and said, "I am beloved, precious child of God, and. . . ." Catching sight of herself in the mirror—hair sticking up, blood and tears streaking her face, dress torn, dirty, and rebuttoned askew, she started again, "I am beloved, precious child of God, and. . . ." She looked in the mirror again and declared, " . . . and God is still working on me. If you come back tomorrow, I'll be so beautiful I'll take your breath away!"

Prayer: Lord, baptize me in the waters of your grace that I might remember always who I am and the One to whom I belong. Amen.[2]

Remember our baptism. On a table, place a bowl of water, and indicate that it represents the waters of baptism.

- Invite participants to come and together dip their fingers in the water as a reaffirmation of God's blessing and the "grace freely bestowed on us in the Beloved."

- Then invite them to turn to the persons on either side of them (one at a time), take their wet hands, and quietly proclaim God's blessing with the words from the reading: "(Name), you are beloved, precious child of God and beautiful to behold!" Offer silent prayer for one another. (Or, have the group say this line in unison for each person.)

- Celebrate God's grace in this moment by singing a hymn such as "Thank You, Lord"; "In God's Image"; "Fear Not, for I Have Redeemed You"; or any baptismal hymn).

Remind everyone of assignments for the coming week, the meeting time and place, and other announcements.

Say or sing a benediction, such as "Shalom to You" or "Companion Song."

Leader's Notes on Scripture Readings

Genesis 1:27—"So God created humankind in his image." Out of divine love, God has created us as we are; we are not mistakes. God celebrates and blesses our creation, saying with complete delight, "It is very good." We are created in community with one another to be mirror images of God's love and freedom to share life, create, give generously of self, and live responsibly and sacrificially for the sake of others. The second-century theologian Irenaeus wrote, "The glory of God is the human being fully alive."

Isaiah 43:1-7—"I have called you by name, you are mine. . . . I will be with you . . . you are precious in my sight, and honored, and I love you." God created us "for [God's] glory" (43:7); God's love and commitment to us cannot be overstated. For the purpose of reflecting divine glory God creates us, forms us, redeems us, names us, and promises to remain with us.

Mark 1:9-11—"A voice came from heaven, 'You are my Son, the Beloved; with you I am well pleased." On one level, this is a story about Jesus' baptism, an event that tells us who Jesus is and tells Jesus who he is! On another level, the story reminds us of our own baptism and tells us who we are "in him." The blessing and empowerment Jesus received here are the very blessing and empowerment God bestows upon us "in the Beloved" (Eph. 1:6). As the writers of Part 1 point out, "Grace is the gift of God's own presence with us, 'freely bestowed on us in the Beloved.'"

Solitary Reflection Exercise

Read Mark 1:9-11 slowly and prayerfully.

Ponder these questions in your journal.

1. The world knew Jesus as "Jesus from Nazareth in Galilee." What do you think it meant to Jesus that God knew him as "my Son, the Beloved; with you I am well pleased"?

2. How does God know you? Use your imagination to get into the river of baptism and stand alongside Jesus in the story. Overhear God's blessing as it applies to you, a blessing Jesus wants to share with you. Translate into your own words what this blessing means for you.

The Flow and the Means of Grace

PREPARATION

Prepare yourself spiritually. Review the introductory material again if you would find this helpful. Read the material for Week 3, do the exercises, and keep your own journal notes. Pray for each participant and for your openness to God as you lead the group.

Prepare the room and materials. Review all Leader's Guide material for this week's meeting. Also review the list of hymns found on page 293 of the Participant's Book (Part 1, p. 65*). You may wish to select other hymns or songs from your tradition to add to the three categories listed. Have adequate hymnals/songbooks, and select appropriate songs for the "Opening" and "Closing." You will also need hymnals for the "Deeper Explorations." Prepare the room arrangement with a simple worship focus area.

Review the intent of this meeting: that participants become more aware of their response to God's active presence through their journeys and of the means of grace by which God comes to them.

Consider the need to extend the session time for Week 4 by reviewing pages 53–54, and let the group members know about the change this week.

OPENING (10 MINUTES)

Welcome all participants personally as they enter.

Set the context.

This meeting gives us time to explore more deeply how we want to move forward in our spiritual journeys. Last week we looked at the meaning of God's grace by which we root our lives in love and grow in Christ. This week we will explore our awareness of God's

---

*(Page numbers in parentheses refer to the individually packaged Participant Books.)

gracious presence throughout our lives, pay attention to our response, and consider the various means by which God comes to us.

Join together in worship.

- Light a candle or offer some other small gesture to signal God's presence in our midst. Invite the group to listen to these words of Julian of Norwich:

  And then [God] showed a little thing, the size of a hazelnut, lying in the palm of my hand, as it seemed to me. It was as round as a ball. I looked at it with the eye of my understanding and thought, What can this be? It was answered generally thus: "It is all that is made." I marveled that it could last, for it was so little that it could suddenly have become nothing. I was answered in my understanding, "It lasts and ever shall, for God loves it." And so everything has being by the love of God.[1]

- Invite all group members to take a moment to place themselves and all of this day's concerns in God's loving hand. Allow several minutes for silence.

- Offer a brief prayer for openness to God's presence in this meeting and in our lives.

- Celebrate God's eternal care by singing "Amazing Grace."

Sharing Insights (45 minutes)

Introduce sharing time (5 minutes).

- Indicate that you will remain together as a whole group for sharing around this question: **How has grace brought you safe thus far, and by what means?** Invite people to draw on their reflections from the daily exercises, especially Exercise 4.

- Give participants a few minutes to look over their journals.

- Encourage them to practice listening for God in each person's reflections.

Share from the daily exercises and reflections (40 minutes).

- As leader, set the tone by sharing first (three to four minutes).

- In the last few minutes, encourage people to pause and pay attention to what they are hearing and seeing inwardly as they listen to one another. What means of grace seemed to surface most often?

Break (10 minutes)

Deeper Explorations (45 minutes)

Review briefly the "faces of grace" described in this week's reading (10 minutes).

- Divide a chalkboard or newsprint into three sections labeled "Prevenient," "Justifying," and "Sanctifying Grace."

- Invite everyone to suggest descriptive words, images, analogies, or Bible stories for each term.

- Then distribute hymnals, and refer participants to the list of hymns on page 293 of the Participant's Book (Part 1, p. 65). Explain that hymnody and singing are important means of grace in the church. Hymns play a deeply formative role in our community and lives regardless of our ability to sing. Many favorite hymns emphasize one of the three faces of grace. Some hymnals are partially organized by these three (or similar) categories.

- Ask group members to open their hymnals and to search for favorite hymns that express one of the faces of grace. If your hymnal is partially organized by these categories, invite everyone to thumb through those sections. Look for stanzas that express important understandings or experiences of one of the faces of grace. Read aloud and sing a few stanzas from songs people love; have fun with it.

Listen to a story of God's amazing grace (10 minutes).

- Included below are accounts of Augustine's conversion and John Wesley's conversion. Choose one account, and read it to the group. Encourage the group to listen with an ear for the faces of grace and for evidence of the means of grace through which God was working.

Augustine

I probed the hidden depths of my soul and wrung its pitiful secrets from it, and when I mustered them all before the eyes of my heart, a great storm broke within me, bringing with it a great deluge of tears. I stood up and left Alypius so that I might weep and cry to my heart's content, for it occurred to me that tears were best shed in solitude. I moved away far enough to avoid being embarrassed even by his presence. He must have realized what my feelings were, for I suppose I had said something and he had known from the sound of my voice that I was ready to burst into tears. So I stood up and left him where we had been sitting, utterly bewildered. Somehow I flung myself down beneath a fig tree and gave way to the tears which now streamed from my eyes, the sacrifice that is acceptable to you. I had much to say to you, my God, not in these very words but in this strain: *Lord, will you never be content? Must we always taste your vengeance? Forget the long record of our sins.* For I felt that I was still the captive of my sins, and in my misery I kept crying "How long shall I go on saying 'tomorrow, tomorrow'? Why not now? Why not make an end of my ugly sins at this moment?"

I was asking myself these questions, weeping all the while with the most bitter sorrow in my heart, when all at once I heard the sing-song voice of a child in a nearby house. Whether it was the voice of a boy or a girl I cannot say, but again and again it repeated the refrain "Take it and read, take it and read." At this I looked up, thinking hard whether there was any kind of game in which children used to chant words like these, but I could not remember ever hearing them before. I stemmed my flood of tears and stood up, telling myself that this could only be a divine command to open my book of Scripture and read the first passage on which my eyes should fall. For I had heard the story of Antony, and I remembered how he had happened to go into a church while the Gospel was being read and had taken it as a counsel addressed to himself when he heard the words *Go home and sell all that belongs to you. Give it to the poor, and so the treasure you have shall be in heaven; then come back and follow me.* By this divine pronouncement he had at once been converted to you.

So I hurried back to the place where Alypius was sitting, for when I stood up to move away I had put down the book containing Paul's Epistles. I seized it and opened it, and in silence I read the first passage on which my eyes fell: *Not in revelling and drunkenness, not in lust and wantonness, not in quarrels and rivalries. Rather, arm yourselves with the Lord Jesus Christ; spend no more thought on nature and nature's appetites.* I had no wish to read more and no need to do so. For in an instant, as I came to the end of the sentence, it was as though the light of confidence flooded into my heart and all the darkness of doubt was dispelled.[2]

John Wesley

On May 24, 1738, Wesley received the assurance of faith he had been seeking. The moment was so important to him that he inserted a lengthy spiritual autobiography at this point in his *Journal*, with eighteen points. This selection picks up at point 12, after Wesley has returned to England from Georgia.

12. When I met Peter Böhler again, he consented to focus the discussion on the issue that I desired, namely, Scripture and experience. I first consulted the Scripture. But when I set aside the glosses of men and simply considered the words of God, comparing them together, endeavoring to illustrate the obscure by the plainer passages, I found they all worked against me. I was forced to retreat to my last hold: that experience would never agree with the *literal interpretation* of those scriptures, nor could I admit it to be true till I found some living witnesses of it. Accordingly, the next day he came again with three others, all of whom testified of their own personal experience that a true living faith in Christ is inseparable from a sense of pardon for all past—and freedom from all present—sins. They added with one mouth that this faith was the gift, the free gift of God; and that he would surely bestow it upon every soul who earnestly and perseveringly sought it. I was now thoroughly convinced. By the grace of God, I resolved to seek it unto the end: 1. By absolutely renouncing all dependence, in whole or in part, upon my own works or righteousness; on which I had really grounded my hope of salvation, though I did not know it, from my youth up. 2. By adding to the constant use of all the other means of grace, continual prayer for this very thing—justifying, saving faith, a full reliance on the blood of Christ shed for me, a trust in him, as my Christ, as my sole justification, sanctification, and redemption.

13. I continued thus to seek it (though with strange indifference, dullness, and coldness, and unusually frequent relapses into sin) till Wednesday, May 24. I think it was about five this morning, that I opened my Testament on those words, *He has given us his precious and very great promises, so that through them you may become participants of the divine nature.* Just as I went out, I opened it again on those words, *You are not far from the kingdom of God.* In the afternoon I was asked to go to St. Paul's. The anthem was, *Out of the depths I cry to you, O Lord. Lord, hear my voice! Let your ears be attentive to the voice of my supplications! If you, O Lord, should mark iniquities, Lord, who could stand? But there is forgiveness with you, so that you may be revered. O Israel, hope in the Lord! For with the Lord there is steadfast love, and with him is great power to redeem. It is he who will redeem Israel from all its iniquities.*

14. In the evening I went very unwillingly to a society at Aldersgate Street, where one was reading Luther's preface to the Epistle to the Romans. About a quarter before nine, while he was describing the change that God works in the heart through faith in Christ, I felt my heart strangely warmed. I felt I did trust in Christ, Christ alone for salvation. And an assurance was given me, that he had taken away *my* sins, even *mine*, and saved *me* from the law of sin and death.[3]

Lead reflection on grace and means of grace in the story (10 minutes).

- What phrases or images stood out in your mind? What faces of grace did you identify in the story?

- What means of grace were involved in the conversion?

- What hymn or song might express the form of God's grace or the human experience that you hear in the story?

Lead reflection on grace and means of grace in the experiences of the group (15 minutes).

- Where does the story of Augustine/Wesley connect in some way with your experience?

- What means of grace have played a special role in your journey, and how?

- Ask each person to locate one hymn or song that best expresses his or her experience of God's grace. Allow the group members time to search for such a hymn and then some time to share where they see meaningful connections.

CLOSING (10 MINUTES)

Take time to pray. Invite listening in silence for the music of the Spirit in your midst.

Select two or three hymns or stanzas of hymns to sing as an expression of praise and worship. Draw on the hymns that were just identified as having special meaning to one or more of the group participants. Read the words if it is difficult to sing in the particular setting where you are meeting.

Close by inviting sentence prayers from those who choose to pray aloud.

Prayerfully review the meeting. What especially touched your mind or heart? Where were you most present to God? Where was your presence to God interrupted?

Announce next week's meeting time and place and any other matters of import to the group.

Say or sing a benediction.

Part 1, Week 4
Sharing Journeys of Faith

PREPARATION

Prepare yourself spiritually. If you need to, review the introductory section on leading small groups for spiritual growth. Read the material for Week 4, do the exercises, and keep your own journal. Pray for each participant and for your availability to God during the upcoming meeting.

Prepare the room and materials. Have hymnals/songbooks ready, and select your songs. Set up your room with a worship focus area. Review the Leader's Guide material for this session. Be prepared to ask how your group wants to deal with the timing issue for this meeting and the next. Prepare to be a timekeeper.

Review the intent of this meeting: that group members discover their own way of seeing and describing their spiritual journeys and that they grow together in Christian community through sharing their stories with one another.

OPENING (10 MINUTES)

Welcome all participants personally as they enter.

Set the context.

- **Last week we explored the ways through which we experience God's presence in our lives. This week we will start to share the fruit of our reflecting on the Christian spiritual life as we tell the stories of our personal journeys.**

- Remind the group that each person will have ten to fifteen minutes to present. (This will give six to eight people time to present in a two-hour meeting frame. A larger group may decide to allot more time for this meeting or to schedule an extra meeting to allow completion of this process. Give the group the opportunity to decide.)

Join together in worship.

- Light a candle to signal God's reality in our midst. Invite the participants to listen or join you in slowly reciting Psalm 23. **Long ago, this was someone's way of telling a story about God's sustaining, guiding presence in his or her spiritual journey. Take a moment silently to give thanks for the ways that God has shepherded us and that we will be hearing about as we share our own journeys.**

- Celebrate God's love and prepare for storytelling by singing a hymn such as "The Lord's My Shepherd"; "My Shepherd, You Supply My Need"; "Bless the Lord"; "Come and Fill" (Taizé); or "Come, Thou Fount of Every Blessing" (note: "ebenezer" is a stone of help, a reminder of what God has done).

- Offer a brief prayer for perceiving God's presence in our stories.

SHARING SPIRITUAL JOURNEYS (1 HOUR AND 40 MINUTES, INCLUDING BREAK)

Introduce the sharing of personal journeys (2 minutes).

- Ask participants to listen as they would to a sacred story or a saga never before told.

- Indicate that after each presentation, group members will have two to three minutes to affirm what they heard.

Present spiritual journeys (45 minutes).

BREAK (8 MINUTES)

Continue to present spiritual journeys (45 minutes).

CLOSING (10 MINUTES)

Pray for each person who presented. For example, invite the group to gather around that person and join hands as you offer a sentence prayer of thanksgiving or intercession for each in turn.

Lead the group in a few minutes of prayerful reflection on the experience of listening and presenting our stories. **What were you aware of as you listened? as you presented? Where did you hear or see God in one another's stories?**

Offer a closing prayer of praise, or sing a benediction.

Living As Covenant Community

PREPARATION

Prepare yourself spiritually. Read the material for Week 5 and complete all the exercises. Pray for each participant and for your presence to God during the meeting.

Prepare the room and materials. Have hymnals/songbooks, and select songs for the "Opening" and "Closing." Arrange the room with chairs in a circle and a worship focus area.

Review the intent of this meeting: that participants become more aware of their response to Christ's call to community and that they develop a covenant of mutual support for this journey as companions in Christ. Even if your group does not plan to move into Part 2 immediately, developing a covenant will help group members continue to care for one another.

OPENING (10 MINUTES)

Welcome all participants personally as they enter.

Set the context.

Last week we listened to stories of one another's spiritual journeys. This week we want to look at what it means to be together in Christ as a community and to develop a covenant of mutual support that can strengthen our common journey.

Join together in worship.

• Light a candle, acknowledging that Christ is the light at the center of our community.

• Dietrich Bonhoeffer wrote in *Life Together*, "Let him who cannot be alone beware of community.... Let him who is not in community beware of being alone. Into the community you were called; the call was not meant for you alone."[1] Invite the group to pause for a few moments of silence and sense being collected in the presence of God who calls us together in Christ.

- Offer a brief prayer for openness to God's guidance in our meeting and our lives.

- Celebrate by singing a hymn such as "Draw Us in the Spirit's Tether," "Ubi Caritas," "We Are One in the Spirit" or "Companion Song."

SHARING INSIGHTS (45 MINUTES)

Introduce sharing time (5 minutes).

- Indicate that you will start sharing around Exercises 1 and 2: **What deeper call and promise do you sense in committing to be part of this journey as companions in Christ? What joys and struggles have you experienced so far?**

- Invite participants to look over their journal entries for a minute or so.

- Encourage them to listen for God in each person's thoughts and experiences.

- As leader, set the tone by sharing first around these two questions.

Share in small groups of three or four (30 minutes).

Allow sharing to develop naturally and to include all exercises, as the Spirit moves the group.

Permit time for group process (10 minutes).

- After sharing, invite a pause to pay attention to what people are hearing and seeing as they listen.

- **What refrains do you hear about our reasons for being part of this group? about the kinds of mutual support we are saying we would cherish or resist?**

- **What has gone well about the way we have been companions in Christ thus far? What do we need to work on?**

BREAK (10 MINUTES)

DEEPER EXPLORATIONS (45 MINUTES)

Introduce the covenanting process (5 minutes).

What we want to do is agree on a few expressions of mutual support and shared practice that will serve as a simple covenant for our journey as companions in Christ. Obviously,

we have already made a number of commitments to be a part of this group—to read and complete the daily exercises, to meet with one another on a weekly basis, to share in a process of honest and mutual discovery. How do we capture in words our commitment to one another and to the process? What other commitments do we want to include? (In general, this process will result in commitments of attitudes, such as openness, willingness, supportive care, listening, and confidentiality, rather than commitments involving additional time. However, the group might wish to consider meeting for up to two and one-half hours to allow for an unhurried process, if all are able and willing.)

Devote time to the covenanting process (30 minutes).

• Invite the group members to focus on their journal entries for Exercises 4 and 5.

• Take turns naming one or two commitments or forms of mutual support you would welcome.

• Gather up all that is being offered by writing it out on chalkboard or newsprint.

• Begin the process of combining, sifting, and refining the list. (Note: Avoid getting bogged down in a group editorial process. Agree on the basic substance. Before the next meeting you or an appropriate participant can volunteer to refine wording in a way that honors the group's intent. If the process is blocked by disagreement, suggest that one aspect of a covenant might be learning to disagree with grace, respect, and a shared commitment to patient, prayerful searching for God's intent.)

Introduce the Companions in Christ Network and prayer connections (10 minutes).

Other groups across the country are participating in *Companions in Christ* as our group is doing. Though we focus on what is happening in our group, we can be connected to other groups engaged in the same spiritual journey. The communication link for us initially is the Web page set up by Upper Room Ministries. Later we may have opportunity to be in direct contact with another group if we choose. The Web address is www.companionsinchrist.org. You can access this site for yourself and read comments from other groups. We make our initial contact by filling in this card (use the card titled "Prayers for Our *Companions in Christ* Group" that is bound into the Leader's Guide) and sending it to Upper Room Ministries. Then our group will be listed on its Web site along with other groups. Moreover, the volunteers and groups that work with The Upper Room Prayer Center will begin to pray for us once they receive our card. We too will have an opportunity to pray for other *Companions in Christ* groups as our study proceeds. Complete the leader's portion of the card by providing your name and your church's mailing address. Please provide a street address rather than a post office box number. Ask each member to sign his or her name (first name is sufficient) as evidence of the group's connection to this larger network of persons.

CLOSING (10 MINUTES)

Enter into silence for two minutes. Invite people to breathe deeply: remember God's presence, relax into grace, and release any tensions that may have surfaced.

Reflect on this experience for a few minutes. **Where do you feel inner confirmation or assurance about our choices? Where do you feel concern? Where are you challenged?**

Invite prayer from the group. Ask for brief prayers that surface from this time together. Close with the Lord's Prayer and sing "Blest Be the Tie That Binds" or "Companion Song."

Tend to final matters. Be sure all are aware of the next meeting time, location, and assignments.

Part 2

Feeding on the Word:
The Mind of Christ

Introductory Leader's Notes for Part 2

*P*art 2 presents scripture as a pathway to formation in the mind of Christ. Your role is to guide the group in exploring classic meditative practices by which spiritual seekers allow the living Word to descend from the head to the heart, and from the heart to the hands in transformed living.

Before you begin preparing for Week 1 of Part 2, take a few minutes to survey the whole of Part 2. Get a feel for the flow of the five weekly readings, the five weekly meetings, and the various practices that you will help your group to experience.

Scan the section called "Preparation" on the first page of all five weeks in Part 2 of the Leader's Guide. Make sure you know ahead of time about anything you need to arrange that will require extra time or effort. If your group is having difficulty in completing the "Sharing Insights" and "Deeper Explorations" sections in the time suggested, you may want to consider adding thirty minutes to your meeting time (from a two-hour to a two- and one-half hour time period). Of course, all participants would need to agree to and support this change.

The test group leaders emphasized the need to schedule at least an hour per week of quality time to study and prepare to lead the weekly meetings, in addition to the time required for doing the "Daily Exercises" in the Participant's Book. If you find the formative approaches to scripture in Part 2 relatively unfamiliar, take plenty of time to practice them personally so that you come prepared inwardly as a "learning leader." The quality of your presence as a group leader will be enhanced by the honesty and humility of a true learner in contrast to the pretense of trying to be a "spiritual master" or expert.

When faced with the challenge of guiding the group into an unfamiliar way of interacting with scripture, avoid the temptation of returning to the safety of more familiar patterns of leading Bible studies and Sunday school discussions. Keep the focus on what God wants to say to us in scripture rather than allowing interesting exchanges of opinions or scholarly commentaries on scripture to dominate and displace prayerful listening.

By now you know who tends to dominate dialogue or to remain quiet. Find creative ways to balance the contributions of more and less talkative members. Try to bring out the insights and gifts of the quieter ones while respecting the natural temperaments of group members—not only for their sake but also for the benefit of the group of which they are valued members. If necessary, challenge dominant personalities to be self-aware and to channel their energies in ways that enhance group interaction. Help everyone remember that the heartbeat of this unique course is not in the talking but in the listening. On occasion, interrupt running dialogues; invite the group members to pause and listen in silence to what they are hearing. After a few moments, ask members to speak from their hearts, turning first to those who have had less to say.

Prior to beginning this section, visit www.companionsinchrist.org for insights or conversations about leading this part. Also print out the list of churches that are journeying through *Companions in Christ*. Choose an appropriate time at the beginning or end of a meeting to place the list before your group for prayer. Celebrate your companionship with other churches that united with you in seeking a deeper experience of God's presence and guidance. Ask members of your group to sign a card, write a personal greeting, or send small gifts (such as bookmarks) to a *Companions in Christ* group in another church as a way of offering encouragement and fostering a spirit of communion between churches.

May God be with you as you guide the group members toward becoming companions in the Word.

Why Do We Call the Bible God's Word?

PREPARATION

Prepare yourself spiritually. Read the material for Week 1 of Part 2, do all the exercises, and keep a journal along with the participants. Pray for each participant and for your group meeting. (If your group is just restarting after a break, review the content and expectations from the Preparatory Meeting.)

Prepare materials and the room. Make sure you have hymnals or songbooks and adequate accompaniment. Select songs for the "Opening" and "Closing." Set chairs in a circle with a center table and candle. Have a copy of the Bible reflection sheets on pages 65–66 for all group members.

Review the intent of this meeting: that participants grow in their appreciation for the transforming power of the Word in scripture and for the practice of spiritual reading so that the words of the Bible become the Word of God to them.

OPENING (10 MINUTES)

Welcome all participants personally as they enter.

Set the context.

This meeting is the first of five in which we will learn ways to "feed on God's Word." As we prayerfully read scripture, we begin to allow the mind of Christ that is expressed in God's Word to shape us more deeply. This week we will focus on the distinction between formational and informational approaches to scripture.

Join together in worship.

- Light a candle to recall the Light that illumines our minds when we listen to scripture with hearts open to the Holy Spirit.

- Read Isaiah 55:1-3. Invite participants to reflect on this passage, using these questions: **What do you thirst for? In what ways do you labor for that which does not satisfy? Listen for the invitation to you in this passage.**

- Sing a few stanzas of a hymn or song celebrating God's Word such as "Break Thou the Bread of Life," "O Word of God Incarnate," or "I Love to Tell the Story."

- Offer a brief opening prayer.

SHARING INSIGHTS (45 MINUTES)

Ask the group members to identify where they have experienced God's presence in their lives this past week.

Invite sharing around the daily exercises. **This week's exercises focused on helping us listen to God's promise of life in the words of scripture.**

- Give participants a moment to look over their journals and share what spoke most deeply to them.

- Encourage them to be listeners: Practice listening for God in each person's reflections and story.

- As leader, model sharing by offering your response first (very briefly) or invite any participant who wishes to do so to begin the sharing.

- After all have shared, invite the group to identify any patterns or themes that surfaced.

BREAK (10 MINUTES)

DEEPER EXPLORATIONS (45 MINUTES)

Explore the difference between informational and formational reading of scripture (10 minutes).

- Explain the difference between informational and formational approaches to scripture. Use the chart "Informational and Formational Reading" in the Participant's Book, page 294 (Part 2, p. 61) and the Leader's Notes on page 64 in discussing these two approaches to reading.

- In informational reading and formational reading, we are asking two kinds of complementary questions:

  Informational. **What do I need to know in order to hear what the ancient author was saying to the people then? What truth(s) does this passage convey about God, people, and Christian faith and life?** Sometimes these questions are more necessary than at other times.

  Formational. **Where does this passage invite me to go deeper, and why? Where does God address my life in this passage? What is God saying to me/us? How am I called to respond to God in prayer, change, or action?**

Lead the group in a Bible study on Luke 4:14-30 (30 minutes).

The reflection sheets found on pages 65–66 will help the group move from an informational reading of scripture to a more formative level of reading and reflecting.

- Distribute the reflection sheets to each person.

- Invite everyone to find a quiet space for twenty minutes of solitary reflection.

- Gather the group to share reflections on the passage. Invite all members to share their responses to the final question: "The Spirit of the Lord is upon me, because he has anointed me to _____."

- Lead the group in a round of sentence prayers to thank God for what we received and to pray for those God's Word has directed us toward. (Give permission for people to pass if they are not comfortable praying aloud.)

Ask the group members to discuss what they learned about the two approaches to scripture (5 minutes).

You might use the following questions: **How is this kind of interaction with scripture similar to or different from your accustomed approach? How would you describe the differences between the informational and the formational approaches? What would help you to enter more deeply into scripture?**

CLOSING (10 MINUTES)

Take time to pray. Invite silent listening for the way the Spirit has brought the Word alive for the group in this time. Bring the silence to a close with the Lord's Prayer.

Prayerfully review the meeting. **What especially touched your mind or heart? When did you feel most present to God, or when did God feel most present to you? How was that sense of presence interrupted? restored?**

Announce the time and place of next week's meeting and other matters of importance.

Say or sing a benediction.

Leader's Notes on Scripture Readings

*W*e have already been sharing about the transforming power of God's Word in scripture. There are two sides to the equation of transformation: the dynamic of God's inspiration in the writing of scripture and the dynamic of God's inspiration in our reading of scripture. In other words, God was active and present when scripture was being written; God is also active and present as we read scripture. Robert Mulholland writes in *Shaped by the Word*, "When we are open to God on our side of the inspirational equation, the creative inspiration of the scripture becomes the productive inspiration of God in our lives. We become an inherent part of the inspiration of the scriptures." [1] We can offer openness to God on our side by practicing a formational approach to scripture. (For more on the topic, see *Shaped by the Word*, revised edition, 49–63.)

The Spirit of the Lord Is upon Me
LUKE 4:14-30

1. Informational Questions

a) Read the passage. What information will help us hear the story as Luke tells it?

b) Review the following notes as a part of your reading.

v. 16—Jesus' custom was not only to worship in the synagogue but also to present his message there.

v. 17—The procedure was for the scroll to be handed to Jesus by the attendant of the synagogue.

vv. 18-19—Jesus defines his mission as the fulfillment of Isaiah 61:1-2 with some variations.

v. 20—Jesus stood to read but would then sit to preach.

v. 23—The people became hostile as the magnitude of Jesus' message hit home.

vv. 26-27—The widow at Zarephath and Naaman the Syrian were not Jews, and yet they knew God's help when Israel did not.

[Notes are adapted from *The New Oxford Annotated Bible*, NRSV (New York: Oxford University Press, 1991), 84 NT.]

c) What do you think Jesus was saying with the words, "The Spirit of the Lord is upon me, because he has anointed me . . ."?

d) What do you think Jesus meant by "Today this scripture has been fulfilled in your hearing"?

e) What do you think Luke wanted readers to understand about Jesus and his mission through the telling of this story?

2. Formational Questions

The most fundamental question we bring to our reading of scripture is: What is God calling us to do and be?

Reread verses 18-19. Hear them now, not as an observer of Jesus, but as a participant in Jesus' life. Hear those words addressed to you as a member of the body of Christ, the church.

a) Select the phrase that you hear most clearly or that seems to claim you. Spend a few minutes pondering its meaning for you. Why did it draw your attention?

b) Consider ways you could enact or embody this word—today, tomorrow, or this week. Share your thoughts with God.

c) As a member of the body of Christ, complete this sentence: "The Spirit of the Lord is upon me, because he has anointed me to _____."
Give thanks to God for the particular way God is inviting you to share in Christ's life.

Part 2, Week 2
Studying Scripture As a Spiritual Discipline

PREPARATION

Prepare yourself spiritually. Read the material for Week 2 of Part 2, do the exercises, and keep a journal along with the participants. Spend time in prayer for openness to the presence of God, and pray for each participant.

Prepare materials and the room. Make sure you have hymnals or songbooks and adequate accompaniment. Select a prayer for illumination and songs for the "Opening" and "Closing." Set chairs in a circle with a center table and candle.

Review the intent of this meeting: that participants learn and practice the ancient art of spiritual reading as a way of approaching scripture and receiving the Word.

OPENING (10 MINUTES)

Welcome all participants personally as they enter.

Set the context.

This is our second meeting to explore ways of receiving spiritual nurture and formation through scripture. Our particular focus this week is on "spiritual reading" as a formational approach to God's Word.

Join together in worship.

- Light a candle and offer a "prayer for illumination" like those that precede the reading of scripture in public worship. Invite participants to take the words of the prayer to heart and open themselves to the grace of the Spirit as they listen to God's Word.

- Read Psalm 119:10-16. Offer a few questions for silent reflection, such as: **How do you treasure God's Word in your heart? What aspects of scripture do you find delight in?**

- Sing a hymn or song that celebrates the Word of God (suggestion: "Jesus Loves Me").

- Offer a brief opening prayer.

SHARING INSIGHTS (45 MINUTES)

Ask the group members to identify where they have experienced God's presence in their lives this week.

Ask the members to select one exercise to share. Allow three to four minutes each.

- Give participants a moment to look over their journals.

- Encourage them to be listeners: Practice listening for God in each person's reflections and story.

- As leader, model sharing by offering your response first (very briefly) or invite any participant who wishes to do so to begin the sharing.

- After everyone has shared, invite the group to identify any patterns or themes that surfaced. Lift up the many ways God speaks to us personally through these ancient texts, in a manner specifically suited to our time and need. This is the grace of the Spirit at work in the scripture.

BREAK (10 MINUTES)

DEEPER EXPLORATIONS (45 MINUTES)

Last week, we discussed the difference between informational and formational approaches to scripture. One name for a formational approach is "spiritual reading." Let's explore what is involved in spiritual reading and then practice it.

Introduce spiritual reading (15 minutes).

- Offer these basic suggestions for spiritual reading of scripture:

  1. The purpose of spiritual reading is to listen to God. Keep asking yourself, "What is God seeking to say to me through all of this?"

  2. Respond to what you read with your heart and spirit as well as with your rational and intellectual faculties. Read scripture as you would read and ponder a letter

from a friend—all within the context of a relationship. Where more explanation is needed, seek it. But do so without losing your focus on the relationship.

3. Let your response take place in the deeper levels of your being. Ask yourself questions such as, "How do I feel about what is being said? How am I responding deep within?" Then explore your responses: "Why am I responding in this way? Where do these feelings come from? What is going on inside me?" Reflect on what your reactions tell you about yourself—your attitudes, habits, perspectives, and relationship with God. As you become more aware of your personal response to the reading, ask, "What is God saying to me here?"

• Invite the participants to build on these suggestions with their insights and experiences. You might ask them to think about the differences between reading the newspaper and reading a personal letter, or between reading a car manual and reading the Bible. How would they characterize the differences in intent, approach, and preparation?

• Read Acts 8:26-40 as an illustration of spiritual reading. Ask the group to look for evidence of spiritual reading and some of its dynamics. **What does the story tell us?**

Guide the group in a spiritual reading, using Acts 8:26-40 (30 minutes).

First, ask someone in the group to read the passage again to the group. Group members can either read along or simply listen (5 minutes).

• Encourage group members to listen this time for the flow of the story and for aspects of the story that may require more explanation or background.

• Share background information as you feel it is needed. Draw on the material in the Leader's Notes on page 71.

Second, direct participants to read and meditate on the passage silently for themselves (15 minutes).

• Ask them to find a space for solitude.

• Remind them to apply the suggestions for spiritual reading.

• Encourage them to leave time for silent reflection on what God is saying to them through this reading experience.

Third, call the group back together for a plenary reflection (10 minutes).

- Invite participants to share one gift they received through this time of spiritual reading.

- Ask them to reflect on what happened and what they did during their reading time: how they approached it, difficulties they experienced, or learnings they had about spiritual reading.

CLOSING (10 MINUTES)

Sing a meditative song or a chant to gather yourselves in a spirit of attentiveness to God. Suggestions include the following: Taizé chants such as "Ubi Caritas," "Bless the Lord," or "Alleluia." Also "Spirit of the Living God"; "Santo, Santo, Santo" (Argentine folk version); or traditional "Holy, Holy, Holy" sung quietly.

Take time to pray. Invite brief prayers for one another that arise naturally from what has been shared in your time together. Close with the Lord's Prayer or a psalm phrase.

Prayerfully review the meeting. **Where did you sense God's presence or guidance in this meeting time? Where or how was that sense interrupted? What grace will you carry with you into your life this week (in a word or phrase)?**

Announce next week's meeting time and place and any other matters of importance.

Say or sing a benediction.

Leader's Notes on Acts 8:26-40

*Y*ou may find it helpful to review these notes in preparation for responding to the kinds of questions that might surface in the first part of this exercise. It is background information only. If participants' questions do not call it all forth, there is no need to present this information.

It was common for court officials of a queen to be eunuchs. Sometimes parents dedicated young children to the court in return for royal favor or protection. An adult eunuch could be distinguished by a high voice, by a plump physique, and often by a shaved head.

Jewish people, part of the Jewish Diaspora (dispersion), were in Ethiopia at that time. The eunuch in this story may have been a "God-fearer" or proselyte, being prepared by intensive instruction to become a Jewish convert.

Deuteronomy 23:1 specifies that a eunuch is not to be admitted to the assembly of God. Historical records indicate that there was a four-foot wall around the Temple in Jerusalem promising death to any Gentile who entered unlawfully. Eunuchs were barred from Temple worship in the Jewish tradition because their "mutilation" rendered them impure or blemished.

However, Isaiah 56:3-5 indicates a promise for the future concerning eunuchs and other "foreigners" that the story in Acts 8 seems to fulfill.

While it is possible that the eunuch had learned some Hebrew, it is more likely that he read and spoke Greek, the common language of the time. He would have been a well-educated man as well as a man of means, given his profession as court treasurer.

Be sure to help participants take note of the text the eunuch is reading, and ask if they see any reason why the eunuch might be particularly interested in it.

Part 2, Week 3
Meditating on the Word

PREPARATION

Prepare yourself spiritually. Read the material for Week 3 of Part 2, do all the exercises, and keep a journal along with the participants. Pray for each participant and for your ability to be present to God in and through the group meeting.

Prepare materials and the room. Make sure you have hymnals or songbooks and adequate accompaniment. If it is not in your hymnal, obtain songbooks, cassette, or CD with Amy Grant's popular song "Thy Word Is a Lamp unto My Feet," if possible. Set chairs in a circle with a center table and candle.

Review the intent of this meeting: that participants continue to learn *lectio divina* as a way of entering into scripture and hearing God's word for their lives.

OPENING (10 MINUTES)

Welcome all participants personally as they enter.

Set the context.

All week we have been practicing a classic way of meditating with scripture called *lectio divina*. In our meeting time this week, we will be deepening our understanding and experience of this form of spiritual reading.

Join together in worship.

- Light a candle. Ask participants to gaze upon the light and inwardly to invite the Holy Spirit to illumine the mind and heart of each person in this meeting as they gather around the sacred text.

- Read Psalm 119:105-12. Offer a few minutes for silent reflection, and then read again verses 105, 111, and 112. Suggest that participants spend a few minutes in silent reflection and prayer.

- Sing or play the song "Thy Word Is a Lamp unto My Feet," perhaps inviting the group to sing the refrain together after each stanza. You may substitute another appropriate song if you cannot obtain the music/words for this piece.

- Offer a brief opening prayer.

Sharing Insights (45 minutes)

Allow time for the participants to talk about where they have experienced God's presence in their lives this past week.

Invite sharing around the daily exercises. The focus this week is on trusting God's abundance and love. Begin the sharing by looking at Exercise 5.

- Give participants a moment to look over their journals and remember their experiences.

- As leader, model sharing by offering your response first (very briefly) or invite any participant who wishes to do so to begin the sharing.

- After all have shared, invite the group to identify any patterns or themes that surfaced.

Break (10 minutes)

Deeper Explorations (45 minutes)

Introduce the practice of lectio divina *(10 minutes).*

Review the background of the ancient practice of Christian meditation called *lectio divina* and the four basic movements. The group has been using this approach to praying the scriptures all week through the daily exercises. Avoid complex and esoteric language. Explain the naturalness of the movements in everyday ways, perhaps noting the ordinary words we might use today to describe each stage: *Read, Reflect, Respond,* and *Rest.*

Lead the group in a guided experience of lectio divina *using Philippians 2:1-11 (35 minutes).*

- Before you begin, ask participants to prepare with a moment of silent opening to God.

- *Read*

  Prepare participants for the first reading by asking them to listen silently as though hearing it for the first time. What parts catch their attention? What words, phrases, or images do they hear as though for the first time? As they listen, ask them to jot these down in their journal and to wait in silence for time to share.

  Read the passage the first time slowly.

  After one to two minutes of silence, invite them to share words, phrases, or images only. (Meanings and interpretations will come later.)

- *Reflect*

  Ask participants to prepare for the second reading and, as they listen, to focus on any particular phrase or image to which they feel drawn. Use these questions: **Why do you feel drawn to it? What does it remind you of? What meaning does it hold for you? What could God be saying to you?**

  Read the passage a second time slowly.

  After two to three minutes, invite them to share in response to the questions.

- *Respond*

  Ask participants to prepare for a third reading. This time, as they listen, invite them to shift from conversing with themselves about the text to conversing with God. Encourage them to tell God what the passage evokes in them, then to listen and respond to what God has to say.

  Read the passage the third time. After three minutes of silence for personal prayer, invite participants to a time of shared prayer. Ask them to lift to God the thanksgiving, concerns, and intercessions that meditation on the text has called forth.

- *Rest*

  Invite participants into a time of silence to rest deeply in God's loving presence. Ask them to release themselves and their prayers to God in childlike trust. Allow several minutes of quiet.

- Lead the group in reflecting on the experience of *lectio divina*. What did they receive? What did they find most helpful about the process? What did they find obtrusive or unnatural? Do they see how the same approach can be used in times of solitary reflection as well as with a group?

CLOSING (10 MINUTES)

Sing together or play once again "Thy Word Is a Lamp unto My Feet." You may choose to sing or play instead another appropriate song such as "The Lord Is My Light" (Taizé).

Enter silence together and consider the prayer-phrase that each of you might carry into the coming week from your *lectio* during this meeting time. Persons may speak the phrase aloud if they wish.

Offer a closing prayer of thanksgiving.

Announce any matters of importance to the group.

Say or sing a benediction.

Part 2, Week 4

Directing Imagination

PREPARATION

Prepare yourself spiritually. Read the material for Week 4 of Part 2, do all the exercises, and keep a journal along with the participants. Pray for each participant and for God's guidance during the meeting.

Prepare materials and the room. Make sure you have hymnals or songbooks and adequate accompaniment. Set chairs in a circle with a center table and candle. For the "Closing," fill a large, edged cookie sheet with sand or dirt.

Review the intent of this meeting: that participants learn new ways to read and meditate on scripture using their imaginations.

OPENING (10 MINUTES)

Welcome all participants personally as they enter.

Set the context.

This week in the reading and daily exercises we have been exploring various ways of meditating with scripture imaginatively. In our meeting time, we will share some of those experiences and work through a guided meditation together.

Join together in worship.

- Light a candle to represent Christ in our midst. Invite participants to visualize the light of Christ radiating from that center into all the room. Lead a brief guided imagery prayer: **With your eyes closed now, imagine this light filling each person, penetrating each mind, blessing each heart with showers of gracious love. . . . Soak up the light and love that surround you; breathe them into every cell of your body, letting them refresh and sustain you. . . . Give thanks inwardly and with your eyes still closed let your** arms or hands or face express your gratitude in any way that feels natural. . . . When your prayer seems complete, open your eyes.

- Sing a hymn or song about the light of Christ. It could be an Advent hymn if this is appropriate to the season of your meeting time. Suggestions include the following: "Christ, Whose Glory Fills the Skies"; "O Splendor of God's Glory Bright"; "Break Forth, O Beauteous Heavenly Light"; "I Am the Light of the World"; "Stay with Us" (Taizé); or "When the Night Becomes Dark" (Taizé).

- Read Psalm 19:7-10 at a gentle pace, and close with a brief prayer asking God to give us hearts to desire God's Word more than fine gold or other worldly treasures.

SHARING INSIGHTS (45 MINUTES)

Invite participants to speak about where God seemed present in their lives during the past week.

Ask members to share their experiences with the daily exercises and especially the experience in using imagination with the familiar stories of Christ's birth.

- Encourage them to be open to what God may be saying through the words and experiences of the other participants.

- As leader, model sharing by offering your response first (very briefly) or invite any participant who wishes to do so to begin the sharing.

- After all have shared, invite the group to identify any patterns or themes that surfaced.

BREAK (10 MINUTES)

DEEPER EXPLORATIONS (45 MINUTES)

Explore the use of the imagination in meditating on scripture.

Discuss people's experience with this week's scripture meditation (10 minutes).

- Ask them to pause for a moment to reflect on how they are doing with using their imagination in meditating on scripture and to identify the following:

  — What has gone well for them?

  — Where have they experienced difficulty?

— Which of the various approaches in this week's exercises seemed easy and fruitful, or difficult and unfruitful?

- Remember that different people find different approaches more suited to them. On the other hand, uncomfortable approaches may tap more deeply into the inner life and bring more transforming power in our lives because they use mental/spiritual "muscles" rarely exercised.

- Remind participants of these words from this week's reading: "By using the imagination, we carry on a conversation with biblical figures and events through which God chose to speak. We try to become a part of the story, picturing it and identifying with the persons described. As we enter into the story this way, it can open up insight, inspire us, and enliven us" (Participant's Book, page 96; Part 2, p. 46).

- Prepare participants for the guided imagery meditation by using some of the information contained in the Leader's Notes (page 82).

Lead the group in a guided imagery meditation based on John 8:2-11 (20 minutes).

- First, read the Bible story aloud and invite participants to list the images that are most vivid for them.

- Then, prepare the group for a guided imagery meditation based on this story by asking all members to listen with eyes closed and to free their imaginations to see, hear, feel, smell, make associations, and participate in the story. Encourage them to keep their journals ready for jotting down discoveries or insights.

- Invite a moment of silence and prayer using these words or similar ones: **Let's offer God our imaginations and mental images for use as creative means of grace and truth in our lives.**

- Lead the group in the following guided imagery meditation. Remember to read slowly. Pause (indicated by ellipses . . .) between questions so participants have time to let questions sink in and reflect on them.

"Early in the morning he came again to the temple. All the people came to him and he sat down and began to teach them."

Visualize the scene. Imagine Jesus coming to the Temple with his disciples, as was his custom day after day. Imagine people gathering about, sitting down around him, as he begins to teach. What do you see? . . . What does it feel like to be here? . . . Why are you here?

"The scribes and the Pharisees brought a woman who had been caught in adultery; and making her stand before all of them, they said to him, 'Teacher, this woman was caught in the very act of committing adultery.'"

Identify with the woman. Who are you, and what is your life like? . . . How do you feel as you are brought before Jesus and made to stand before all of them? . . . How do you feel about your accusers? . . . How does Jesus look at you as they bring you forward?

"They said to him, 'Teacher, this woman was caught in the very act of committing adultery. Now in the law Moses commanded us to stone such women. Now what do you say?' They said this to test him, so that they might have some charge to bring against him."

Identify with one of the scribes or Pharisees. How do you feel about what you are doing right now? . . . How do you feel about this woman? . . . How does Jesus look at you as you bring her forward and make your charge?

"Jesus bent down and wrote with his finger on the ground. When they kept on questioning him, he straightened up and said to them, 'Let anyone among you who is without sin be the first to throw a stone at her.' And once again he bent down and wrote on the ground."

How do you respond to what Jesus said?

Now identify with Jesus. As you look at the Pharisees and the woman, what do you see as the real issue here? . . . When you bend over, what do you write on the ground?

"When they heard it, they went away, one by one, beginning with the elders; and Jesus was left alone with the woman standing before him."

Let yourself become the woman again. How does it feel to be standing alone before Jesus?

"Jesus straightened up and said to her, 'Woman, where are they? Has no one condemned you?' She said, 'No one , sir.' And Jesus said, 'Neither do I condemn you. Go your way and from now on do not sin again.'"

What thoughts and feelings do Jesus' words stir up in you? . . . What do you want to say to Jesus before you go on your way?

Offer a few moments afterward for solitary reflection (5 minutes). Invite group members to make notes in their journals about their experience.

Debrief the experience in the total group (10 minutes).

- Lead a brief discussion using some questions such as these:

  What accusation do you feel hangs over you today?

  Who do you feel needs to be stoned today?

  Whom have you judged, and could you let go of the judgment?

  What difficult situations are you being asked to resolve? What path would Jesus take?

- Discuss the process: what participants found helpful, difficult, or unhelpful about the use of the imagination in meditating on the story.

CLOSING (10 MINUTES)

Participate in the forgiveness Jesus offers in the story.

- Prepare for worship by placing a large, edged cookie sheet filled with sand or dirt on the ground before everyone—a reminder of the ground on which Jesus wrote with his finger.

- Invite the group to listen to or sing prayerfully the Taizé song "Lord Jesus Christ" from the CD titled *Sing to God* or another hymn that you select.

- Give all participants an opportunity to come forward, as they desire, to write in the sand a letter or image that represents an accusation of themselves or someone else for which they need release and forgiveness. (As persons come forward, encourage the group to continue praying with the song.)

- After each person draws something in the sand, brush your hand over the sand so as to erase what he or she has written, while quoting John 8:11: "Jesus said, 'Neither do I condemn you. Go your way, and from now on do not sin again.'"

- Offer a benediction.

Prayerfully review the meeting. **Where did you feel most present to God? Where was that sense of presence broken or displaced? What gift do you take with you into the coming week?**

Announce any matters of importance to the group.

As a closing benediction, read Psalm 19:14.

Leader's Notes on Guided Imagery Meditations

SOME GUIDELINES

1. Remember that throughout the Bible, God speaks to people through images. Keep the focus on what the God of Jesus Christ wants to reveal through images, not images for their own sake. Be prepared for surprises as God meets us in imaginative interplay with scripture.

2. Recognize that people will "see" these meditations differently. Everyone brings personal memory of life-images to scripture. Also, some people get a clear picture; others do not, and they may have difficulty with this approach.

3. Do not be overly concerned that people follow a meditation precisely. In the course of a meditation, a person may be inclined to follow another image or go in a different direction that may express God's particular leading for that individual. Tell the group in advance that it is all right if this happens.

WHEN LEADING OTHERS

When guiding others, begin by leading them in a moment of silence and inward prayer. Then, in a spoken prayer, offer your imaginations and mental images to God as creative means for conveying grace and truth in your life. Read one portion of the meditation at a time slowly. *Pause between statements or suggestions.* Give people enough time to visualize scenes you are describing, to make a transition from one thought to another, and to let their imaginations bring forth responses to your prompts. Prepare your spirit and discover a helpful pace by leading yourself through the meditation ahead of time. In this way, you lead others into an internal process you have already experienced.

WHEN LEADING YOURSELF

Begin with a moment of silence and prayer. Offer your imagination and mental images to God. Read one portion at a time, then close your eyes and take up the thoughts or images with your imagination. Rather than manufacturing responses, allow time for responses to arise from within and even to surprise you. Walk yourself slowly through the meditation in this manner. If nothing seems to be happening, explore what the "nothing" is. Is an emotion, leftover business, or a daydream occupying your mind? Can you let it go? Are you allowing a distraction to prevent you from seeing, feeling, or dealing with something? Afterward, take time to make notes about insights, feelings, responses, surprises, or blocks.

Part 2, Week 5
Group Meditation with Scripture

PREPARATION

Prepare yourself spiritually. Read the material for Week 5 of Part 2, do all the exercises, and keep a journal along with the participants. Spend time in prayer for each participant and also pray that you might hear God speaking to you through the interaction with the group.

Prepare materials and the room. Make sure you have hymnals or songbooks and adequate accompaniment. Plan to have several candles for the "Opening," and select your songs in advance. Set chairs in a circle with a center table and candles.

Review the intent of this meeting: that participants learn and practice group *lectio* as a way of being together in the Word.

OPENING (10 MINUTES)

Welcome all participants as they enter.

Set the context.

Throughout these five weeks, we have been exploring various ways in which scripture serves as a means of grace and guidance in our lives. In this final meeting, we will experience one more simple and fruitful way of using *lectio* in a small group.

Join together in worship.

- Light a candle to represent Christ in our midst. Light several smaller candles or votives to represent our lives in Christ, shining with grace. Cluster the smaller candles around the center candle. Note how much more light there is when we gather in community around our risen Lord.

- Invite intercessory prayer through imagination: **Close your eyes and visualize God's tremendous uncreated light, the very light of Life. . . . Now see a person you have a special concern for, and bring that person into God's healing light. . . . Hold this person in the light, and imagine divine peace, cleansing, forgiveness, and restoration entering into every layer of the person's being. . . . Release this person now into God's gracious care for the future. Bring your prayer to a close, and open your eyes.**

- Sing a hymn or song that relates to the healing power of God's incarnate Word such as "There Is a Balm in Gilead"; "Spirit Song"; "Healer of Our Every Ill"; or "Praise, My Soul, the King of Heaven."

SHARING INSIGHTS (45 MINUTES)

Take some time for participants to share how God has been a part of their lives during the past week.

Invite sharing around the daily exercises.

- Give participants a moment to look over their journals and then talk about the approach to scripture they chose to use.

- As leader, model sharing by offering your response first (very briefly) or invite any participant who wishes to do so to begin the sharing.

- After all have shared, invite the group to identify any patterns or themes that surfaced.

BREAK (10 MINUTES)

DEEPER EXPLORATIONS (45 MINUTES)

Introduce Norvene Vest's process for group lectio *(10 minutes).*

Group *lectio* is a process for praying the scripture in small groups. Group *lectio* provides a way for groups to make meditation with scripture the center of their meeting time. This type of prayerful meditation is a communal expression of the deep personal intimacy with God that is at the heart of Christian faith. Explain the *lectio* process by using the process guide printed on page 295 of the Participant's Book (Part 2, p. 62).

Guide a group lectio *experience using Luke 5:1-11 (30 minutes).*

- Assign three persons in addition to yourself to be readers. You, the leader, will be Reader #1. Ask the readers to read slowly when you give them the signal so listeners can hear each word and phrase. Remind listeners before each reading what to pay attention to. Prepare the group members by asking them to become quiet and present to God, waiting in expectancy.

- Remind members to listen for overall comprehension. When you are ready, read the passage the first time. (After a few moments of silence, the leader gives guidance for the second reading.)

- Ask each person to listen attentively for a particular word or phrase that seems to be given to each. Reader #2 reads the passage again. Then after a minute of silence, the leader invites persons to speak aloud the word received. (In a spirit of receptivity, the group listens without comment. When everyone has shared, the leader gives guidance about the third reading.)

- Ask the group members to ponder how the passage seems to touch their lives. Reader #3 reads the same passage again. Then each member briefly speaks aloud his or her sense of being touched. (Again, the group receives these words without comment. When appropriate, the leader will give guidance about the fourth reading.)

- Ask the group members to reflect on a possible invitation found in the passage to do or be something in the next few days. Reader #4 reads the same passage yet again. Let each person speak of his or her own sense of invitation. Group responses are limited to questions of clarification or brief affirmations, if deeply felt.

- When all have shared, the leader invites the group to a period of prayer. Each person prays aloud for the person on his or her right—for empowerment to follow through on the invitation. Move around the prayer circle to the left, as each person prays for the person on the right. Group members may pass at any point of sharing in this process. If a person passes on praying aloud, he or she should pray silently and squeeze the hand of the next person when the silent praying is finished.

Lead group reflection on the process (5 minutes).

Let group members share their reactions and any new learnings.

CLOSING (10 MINUTES)

Sing together a hymn or song of your choosing that relates to the themes of this week. You might ask participants for suggestions.

Read Isaiah 55:10-11. Invite participants into silent reflection with a few questions: **The Word that goes forth from God does not return "empty" but fulfills its purpose. How have you experienced the "fullness" of God's Word in these past several weeks? What feelings, words, or images capture your sense of this fruitfulness?** Invite participants to share, if they choose, one word or image from their reflection.

Prayerfully review the meeting. **Where did you sense God's presence or guidance most clearly? Where was this presence obscured for you?**

Announce any matters of importance to the group including the time and place of your next meeting, especially if you are planning to take a break between parts.

Say or sing a benediction.

Part 3

Deepening Our Prayer:
The Heart of Christ

Introductory Leader's Notes for Part 3

*P*art 3 presents prayer as a pathway of spiritual formation in the heart of Christ. Enjoy your role as a learner and as a guide on this six-week adventure in practicing the presence of God in the midst of life!

Before you begin preparing for Week 1 of Part 3, take some time to survey the whole of Part 3. Get a sense for the flow of the six meetings and the various practices that you will facilitate in the "Deeper Explorations" and "Closings."

Scan the section called "Preparation" on the first page of all six weeks in Part 3 of the Leader's Guide for anything that may require you to plan ahead. In particular, note that the "Deeper Explorations" of Week 4 presents you with two options. Either option requires some advance preparation. If you choose option 1, then you may want to start now to collect pictures or art of human situations. If you choose option 2, you will need to make arrangements for a short field trip.

Make part of your weekly preparation a self-directed experience of the "Deeper Explorations" prayer exercise. In this way, you can approach each session with inner confidence in the process and a greater awareness of God's active presence to each person.

Anticipate the appreciation that group members feel for the opportunity to deal with their experiences of prayer and to explore dimensions of our spiritual tradition that they may have heard little about in church or church school. You may want to remind your group that one purpose of this course is to reintroduce vital aspects of classical Christian spiritual practice that belong to all Christians but have been lost along the way, especially in modern Protestant churches. If any participants struggle with more contemplative prayer forms, give them permission to express their concerns and to pray as they can. At the same time, encourage them to enter into these six weeks experimentally, exploring ways they can be present to God and God to them while in the company of trusted friends.

Keep in mind that when you introduce periods of silence for prayer, such as in the "Deeper Explorations" of Weeks 1 and 6 , you are giving your group a wonderful gift. Some degree of resistance is natural in a society that strives to eliminate silence, especially in a group setting. But maintain your course and allow your group to learn by experience the value of voluntary silence with others who are turning their attention to God. Remember that the larger purpose of this course is to provide space for people to practice God's presence, not merely to talk about it.

Prior to beginning this section, visit www.companionsinchrist.org for insights or conversations about leading this part. Also print out the list of churches who are journeying through *Companions in Christ*. Choose an appropriate time at the beginning or end of a meeting to place the list before your group for prayer. Celebrate your companionship with other churches that united with you in seeking a deeper experience of God's presence and guidance. Ask members of your group to sign a card, write a personal greeting, or send small gifts (such as bookmarks) to a *Companions in Christ* group in another church as a way of offering encouragement and fostering a spirit of communion between churches.

Schedule at least an hour per week of quality time to study and prepare for leading the sessions.

May God be with you as you guide the group toward becoming companions in prayer.

Prayer and the Character of God

PREPARATION

Prepare yourself spiritually. Read the material for Week 1 of Part 3, do all the exercises, and keep a journal along with the participants. Pray for a growing attentiveness to God's presence in your life and in the life of each participant.

Prepare materials and the room. Gather art materials, including modeling clay or play dough. If you wish to play meditative music during the time for "practicing the presence of God," select an audiocassette or CD and be sure to bring a music player to the meeting. Select songs and have appropriate hymnals or songbooks for use. Arrange the room for your group with a center table and candle.

Review the intent of this meeting: that participants become more aware of their images of prayer and their actual experience of being present to God.

OPENING (10 MINUTES)

Welcome all participants personally as they enter.

Set the context.

This meeting is the first of six sessions to help us deepen our prayer and, in so doing, enter more fully into the heart of Christ. We begin this week by exploring our images and experiences of prayer.

Join together in worship.

- Light a candle to represent Christ in our midst who leads us from our current understanding and practice to more complete insight and communion in prayer.

- Read a single verse, Luke 11:1. Invite a few minutes of silence to reflect on the disciple's request and to become aware of the nature of our own request as we embark on these sessions of deepening our prayer. Ask participants if they would be willing to share in a word or phrase what they seek from the risen Lord in relation to their prayer life.

- Sing a prayer in the form of a familiar song that invites remembrance of God's living presence such as "Kum Ba Yah," "Spirit of the Living God," or "Surely the Presence of the Lord."

Sharing Insights (45 minutes)

Ask the group members to identify where they have experienced God's presence in their lives this past week.

Invite sharing around the daily exercises.

- Give participants a moment to look over their journals and identify what spoke most deeply to them.

- Encourage them to be listeners: Practice listening for God in each person's reflections and story.

- As leader, model sharing by offering your response first (very briefly) or invite any participant who wishes to do so to begin the sharing.

- After all have shared, invite the group to identify any patterns or themes that surfaced.

Break (10 minutes)

Deeper Explorations (45 minutes)

Introduce the theme of exploring the nature of prayer (5 minutes).

- The reading for this week suggests that prayer is a personal response to God who is already present to us.

- The author of Part 3 writes that in prayer, "We choose to become present to God who is always present to us, and to respond to the One who continually seeks to communicate with us." Read the following quotation from Brother Lawrence on practicing the presence of God.

> I occupy myself solely with keeping myself in God's holy presence. I do this simply by keeping my attention on God and by being generally and lovingly aware of [God]. This

could be called practicing the presence of God moment by moment, or to put it better, a silent, secret, and nearly unbroken conversation of the soul with God.[1]

Engage the group in exploring prayer in the life of Jesus (15 minutes).

• Form pairs and assign each pair one of the following passages about prayer in the life of Jesus: Matthew 11:25-26; Mark 1:35-37; Luke 2:48-51; 22:41-44; John 11:41-44 or John 17:15-23.

• Ask each pair to consider what the passage says or implies about God's presence to Jesus and/or how Jesus was present to God.

• Allow time for the pairs to report back to the full group.

Invite participants to a period of practicing the presence of God—being attentive and present to the reality of God's presence with us (15 minutes).

• **We have explored our thoughts on what it means to be present to God; now we are going to explore our experience.**

• **Take the next fifteen minutes to be quietly present to God in whatever way you feel led (sitting, walking, observing nature, drawing, shaping play dough, journaling, etc.).**

• **We will gather back in fifteen minutes for some sharing.**

• **(Make play dough and art materials available. You may choose to play meditative music in the background, such as music from Taizé.)**

Gather for sharing (10 minutes).

• Form triads.

• Direct them to respond to these questions:

   How would you describe your experience of being present to God?

   What helps you be present to God?

   What interrupts your presence to God?

• Move back into the larger circle and share any learnings or insights with the whole group.

Closing (10 minutes)

Remind the group of assignments, time and place of next meeting, and any other announcements.

Invite each person to name the gift and challenge of the meeting.

Offer a closing prayer, or sing a fitting hymn/song.

Say or sing a closing benediction.

Part 3, Week 2

Dealing with Impediments to Prayer

PREPARATION

Prepare yourself spiritually. Read the material for Week 2 of Part 3, do all the exercises, and keep a journal along with the participants. Pray for each participant and for your leadership, that you may be open to the guidance of the Holy Spirit.

Prepare materials and the room. Select songs or hymns for this session. Make sure you have appropriate hymnals or songbooks. Arrange chairs around a center table and candle.

Review the intent of this meeting: that participants become more aware of their impediments to prayer and have the opportunity to develop a personal breath prayer.

OPENING (10 MINUTES)

Welcome all participants personally as they enter.

Set the context.

This is the second meeting of six on deepening our prayer, which unites us more fully with the heart of Christ. We will continue to explore the theme of blocks or impediments to prayer and try out a particular form of prayer that may be new to us.

Join together in worship.

- We light a candle to help us remember that the risen Christ in our midst is the One we turn to for illumination in prayer. Christ can help us perceive our blocks to the relationship of prayer we desire; Christ can give us courage, hope, persistence, and willingness to move beyond these blocks.

- Sing a song or hymn of assurance, trust, or hope in God such as "The Lord's My Shepherd," "Near to the Heart of God," or "I Will Trust in the Lord." Or, read in unison Psalm 23.

- Offer a prayer for guidance from and receptivity to the Spirit.

SHARING INSIGHTS (45 MINUTES)

Ask the group members to identify where they have experienced God's presence in their lives this past week.

Invite sharing around the daily exercises.

- Give participants a moment to look over their journals and identify what spoke most deeply to them.

- Encourage them to be listeners: Practice listening for God in each person's reflections and story.

- As leader, model sharing by offering your response first (very briefly) or invite any participant who wishes to do so to begin the sharing.

- Ask people to share about the impediments to prayer in their lives.

- After all have shared, invite the group to identify any patterns or themes that surfaced.

BREAK (10 MINUTES)

DEEPER EXPLORATIONS (45 MINUTES)

Introduce the theme of exploring impediments to meditation and prayer (5 minutes).

- Adele Gonzalez writes in our reading for this week, "Praying is not always easy, natural, or spontaneous. If we take our prayer life seriously, we will likely experience times when praying becomes a challenge and a struggle. Many things . . . can come between us and our prayer. It helps to look at these and see what we can learn from them about ourselves and our relationship with God."

- As the weekly reading suggests, impediments can be both external (time, place, interruptions) and internal (preoccupation, resistance, fear, poor images of God). An impediment can also be a need for guidance in how to pray and how to draw on the resources for prayer that God gives us.

(Special note: Discuss the impediments only to the extent that this issue still needs attention following the time of "Sharing Insights.")

Invite participants to a time of meditation and prayer guided by the words of Mark 10:46-52 (25 minutes).

- Set a context by discussing what Dietrich Bonhoeffer wrote in *Life Together*, "The most promising method of prayer is to allow oneself to be guided by the word of the Scriptures, to pray on the basis of a word of Scripture. In this way we shall not become victims of our own emptiness."[1] He went on to say, "Prayer means nothing else but the readiness and willingness to receive and appropriate the Word."[2] **We will be using a passage of scripture to guide us toward discovering the prayer of our hearts and any obstacles to it.**

- Biblical note: **This story is the conclusion to a section of Mark that focuses on true discipleship. Ironically, Mark presents Bartimaeus (not the sons of Zebedee who seek greatness) as the model of true discipleship. The story ends by saying that Bartimaeus followed Jesus "on the way." Our purpose in prayer is to follow Jesus on the way and to grow in his likeness in the process.**

- First reading: Read the story slowly to help the listeners gain a sense of the whole story. Ask group members to name words or images that catch their attention but to name them without elaboration or explanation.

- Second reading: Now invite each person to move slowly through the story of Bartimaeus. Read the story aloud verse by verse. Follow each verse with questions and guidance for focused meditation and prayer as outlined below. (The verses are printed so you will not need to move back and forth from the Bible reading to the meditation questions.)

Read verse 46: "They came to Jericho. As he and his disciples and a large crowd were leaving Jericho, Bartimaeus son of Timaeus, a blind beggar, was sitting by the roadside." *Get in touch with the part of you that is lying by the roadside with Bartimaeus. This may be a forgotten part of you that has been neglected or unattended.* (Pause forty-five seconds.)

Read verse 47: "When he heard that it was Jesus of Nazareth, he began to shout out and say, 'Jesus, Son of David, have mercy on me!'" *What is the persistent cry of your heart?* (Pause forty-five seconds.)

Read verse 48: "Many sternly ordered him to be quiet, but he cried out even more loudly, 'Son of David, have mercy on me!'" *What voices around you and within you tell you to "be quiet" regarding your spiritual hunger?* (Pause forty-five seconds.)

Read verse 49: "Jesus stood still and said, 'Call him here.' And they called the blind man, saying to him, 'Take heart; get up, he is calling you.'" *What voices encourage you toward God, saying, "Take heart; get up, he is calling you"?* (Pause forty-five seconds.)

Read verse 50: "So throwing off his cloak, he sprang up and came to Jesus." *What "cloaks" do you need to throw off in order to spring up and move toward Jesus?* (Pause forty-five seconds.)

Read verse 51: "Then Jesus said to him, 'What do you want me to do for you?' The blind man said to him, 'My teacher, let me see again.'" *Search your heart for your response to Jesus' question, "What do you want me to do for you?" What do you need in order to be whole?* (Pause sixty to ninety seconds.)

Read verse 52: "Jesus said to him, 'Go; your faith has made you well.' Immediately he regained his sight and followed him on the way." *What do you need to do to receive what Jesus wants to give you? What do you need in order to follow him on the way?* (Pause forty-five seconds.)

- Conclude the time by reading the following prayer by Richard of Chichester (1197–1253):

  Thanks be to you, Lord Jesus Christ, for all the benefits which you have won for us, for all the pains and insults which you have borne for us. O most merciful Redeemer, Friend and Brother, may we know you more clearly, love you more dearly, and follow you more nearly day by day. Amen.[3]

- Give the group members a few more minutes to reflect in their journals on this experience and their discoveries. Ask them to think about what they learned about their impediments to prayer and their readiness to receive the life that Jesus wants to give them.

- Ask the group to meet in triads and take turns sharing their discoveries.

Introduce the breath prayer (15 minutes).

- Instruct participants to turn to pages 296–97 in the Participant's Book (Part 3, pp. 81–83,) and find "Developing Your Breath Prayer."

- Explain that a breath prayer is an ancient way of practicing the presence of God, cultivating a posture of constant awareness and availability toward God.

- Explain briefly how to develop a breath prayer. If you are personally familiar with the breath prayer, share your experience.

- Ask everyone to work alone for a few minutes on developing a breath prayer for himself or herself, following the guidance of the material in the Participant's Book. Answer questions or offer guidance as requested.

- Invite everyone to pray his or her breath prayer in silence for three minutes.

CLOSING (10 MINUTES)

Lead the group into a period of silent prayer.

- Invite participants to form pairs. Ask them to share their breath prayers with each other, along with any brief explanation of the prayer if they so choose.

- Then invite pairs to take each other's hands and to pray each prayer in turn, softly repeating the words together several times so that they are retained in memory. Then move to silent prayer.

- When the room has fallen silent for a little while, bring the prayer to closure by saying "Amen" or by starting softly a familiar song the group can join in singing, such as "Breathe on Me, Breath of God" or "Ubi Caritas."

Encourage participants to practice praying their breath prayers through the week. Ask them also to pray for their partner daily by using the partner's breath prayer.

Invite responses to the meeting: **What gifts or challenges were received?**

Say or sing a benediction.

Part 3, Week 3
Prayers of Petition and Intercession

PREPARATION

Prepare yourself spiritually. Read the material for Week 3 of Part 3, do all the exercises, and keep a journal along with the participants. Pray that God will prepare you and each participant to receive the greatest benefit from your group meeting.

Prepare materials and the room. Select songs and gather hymnals/songbooks. Arrange the room, making sure there is sufficient space for small groups of four to form later in the meeting. Set chairs in a circle with a center table and candle.

Review the intent of this meeting: that participants deepen their understanding of intercessory prayer and engage in intercessory healing prayer for one another.

OPENING (10 MINUTES)

Welcome all participants personally as they enter.

Set the context.

This meeting is the third of six sessions on the nature and practice of prayer. In deepening our prayer life, we become more fully united to the heart of Christ. This week we will be expanding our understanding and practice of intercessory prayer. Intercession is a wonderful way of joining our hearts and wills to Jesus Christ, the great Intercessor.

Join together in worship.

- Light a candle to represent Christ in our midst, and invite silent reflection on the truth written in Hebrews 7:25: "He is able for all time to save those who approach God through him, since he always lives to make intercession for them." Pause, and then repeat this phrase. Invite participants to visualize Christ interceding for them personally in some way.

- After a minute of silence, invite participants to speak the names of persons for whom they have been praying this week. Let them speak all together (not in sequence), so they can hear the sound of many voices and names. Then encourage them to "see" Jesus as he hears and receives all these prayers and presents them to God through his own pure mercy and love.

- Sing a song of thanks or confidence such as "Spirit Song"; "Precious Lord, Take My Hand"; or "Thank You, Lord."

SHARING INSIGHTS (45 MINUTES)

Ask the group members to identify where they have experienced God's presence in their lives this past week.

Invite sharing around the daily exercises.

- Give participants a moment to look over their journals and identify what spoke most deeply to them.

- Encourage them to be listeners: Practice listening for God in each person's reflections and story.

- As leader, model sharing by offering your response first (very briefly) or invite any participant who wishes to do so to begin the sharing.

- After all have shared, invite the group to identify any patterns or themes that surfaced.

BREAK (10 MINUTES)

DEEPER EXPLORATIONS (45 MINUTES)

Set a context for a guided experience of intercessory prayer based on Mark 2:1-12 (10 minutes).

- Read Mark 2:1-12 aloud for the group. Invite the participants to focus on verses 1-5.

- Invite the group to discuss briefly some of the connections between this story and the nature of intercessory prayer. Avoid a long, drawn-out Bible discussion of every aspect of the story. Stay focused on how this passage sets a context for intercessory prayer. Some possible insights include the following:

  a) Sometimes we have no faith for ourselves; we need others to have faith for us. In healing the paralytic, Jesus honors the faith and love of the four for their friend.

b) The role of the four was not to cure their friend but to care for him and to carry him into the healing presence of Jesus. That is our role in ministry and in intercessory prayer.

c) The care of the four was evident in their active willingness to go out of their way for their friend and to persevere in love for their friend. Love (not our diagnosis or instructions to God) is the content of prayer for others. We unite our spirits with Christ to be means by which God loves the world.

d) There are factors in and among us (the crowd, the cynics, the roofing) that keep people from God, that obstruct love and intercession, so prayer requires a love that perseveres.

Lead the group in intercessory prayer guided by images from this story (20 minutes).

- Ask everyone to find a comfortable place to sit or lie down, to enter into an attitude of prayer.

- Acknowledge that God is with us and invites us to offer ourselves as vessels for God's presence to others.

- Assure the participants that it is all right to follow their own way of reflecting if they have difficulty visualizing what is being suggested.

- After another moment of silence, guide their prayer with directions like these:

"Imagine yourself as one of the four holding a corner of a stretcher. Now take note of who God places on the stretcher for you to help carry. Who is God calling you to care for, to help carry into God's presence today? Take a moment to see the person and receive him or her in love." (*Pause thirty seconds.*)

"Imagine yourself carrying your friend toward Jesus. In what ways do you feel the path for your friend is obstructed? In what ways are you frustrated in your effort to care for this person? Who or what gets in the way?" (*Pause thirty seconds.*)

"Now imagine yourself persevering in your intent to care for your friend and to bring your friend into Jesus' presence. Dig through the roofing separating your friend and you from Jesus and the healing your friend needs. Are there many layers? What are they?" (*Pause thirty seconds.*)

"Lower your friend into Jesus' presence. Watch and see how Jesus receives your friend, what he does and what he says. See your friend being restored to wholeness in the radiance of divine love." (*Pause one minute.*)

"Release your friend to God's care. Give thanks to God. Return to your home." (*Pause one minute* and say "Amen.")

- Give the group members a few more minutes in silence to reflect on their prayer and to write in their journals.

- Ask the participants to turn to another person to share something they received or something that caused them to struggle.

Invite the group to enter into a second experience of prayer: silent healing prayer for one another (15 minutes).

- Set a context: **We are accustomed to praying for one another with many words, but words can hinder as well as help the flow of God's love. Perhaps you would like to be on that stretcher, carried by friends to Jesus. You will have that opportunity now, if you choose.**

- Form groups of four or five. Guide them as simply as possible.

- Sit in circles with an empty chair in the center of each.

- As a person wishes to be "on the stretcher" and be carried into Jesus' restorative presence, he or she goes and sits in the center chair. The person may express a need aloud if desired, but there is no necessity to do so.

- Group members stand and silently place their hands on the person's head and shoulders and carry the person into Jesus' presence in the prayer of their hearts. No prayers are spoken.

- After a few minutes, the person in the center signals readiness to stand, and all return to their seats. This pattern continues until everyone who chooses to has had a chance to present himself or herself for prayer.

- Emphasize at the outset that it is okay to participate without choosing to sit in the center chair for prayer.

CLOSING (10 MINUTES)

Sing quietly a song of confidence, peace, or healing. (See the list of suggestions from the "Opening.")

Invite brief reflections on, or responses to, the experience of being prayed for and praying for one another in the small groups.

Invite thanksgivings and celebrations for the ways the group experienced Christ's presence.

Say or sing a benediction.

Part 3, Week 4
Praying As We Are

PREPARATION

Prepare yourself spiritually. Read the material for Week 4 of Part 3, do all the exercises, and keep a journal along with the participants. Spend time in prayer seeking God's guidance for the group meeting, and pray for each participant.

Prepare materials and the room. If you choose option 1, collect from magazines and books a sufficient number of pictures or art that depict people and human situations so that each group member, including you, can select one. If you choose option 2, be sure the group members understand the need for additional time. Choose songs and secure the appropriate hymnals or songbooks. Set chairs in a circle with a center table and candle.

Review the intent of this meeting: that participants celebrate their freedom to pray as they can and that they learn to combine prayer and action.

OPENING (10 MINUTES)

Welcome all participants personally as they enter.

Set the context.

This meeting is the fourth of six sessions for deepening our prayer and, in so doing, entering into the heart of Christ. The theme of this meeting is celebrating the way we pray and praying in the midst of action.

Join together in worship.

- Light a candle to represent Christ in our midst as we gather in prayer. Read 1 Thessalonians 5:16-19.

- Sing a song that celebrates our differences and our unity in Christ such as "Many Gifts, One Spirit" or "Weave."

- Offer a prayer on behalf of the group, or invite each group member to offer a one-sentence prayer aloud and indicate that you will conclude the prayer time.

SHARING INSIGHTS (45 MINUTES)

Ask the group members to identify where they have experienced God's presence in their lives this past week.

Invite sharing around the daily exercises.

- Ask group members to select an exercise and to share from their journals. Also ask people to share about the spiritual types with which they identify.

- Give participants a moment to look over their journals.

- Encourage them to be listeners: Practice listening for God in each person's reflections and story.

- As leader, model sharing by offering your response first (very briefly) or invite any participant who wishes to do so to begin the sharing.

- After all have shared, invite the group to identify any patterns or themes that surfaced.

BREAK (10 MINUTES)

DEEPER EXPLORATIONS (45 MINUTES, OPTION 1; 65 MINUTES, OPTION 2)

Guide a brief discussion on new discoveries about the spiritual types described in the reading for this week (5 minutes). Skip this topic if the previous time of sharing generated sufficient discussion.

- Celebrate any discoveries or insights people have into their unique styles of prayer.

- The message of this week's reading could be summed up in this way: pray as you can, not as you think you ought.

- Explain, if necessary, that we might characterize the four spiritual types as head, heart, mystic, and active. They represent different styles of relating to God in prayer. We lift up these types not so we can put ourselves in category boxes but to celebrate the way we relate to God most freely and authentically. Through exploring the four types, we might also discover new ways that God is seeking to communicate and commune with us.

Set a context for an exercise to explore prayer as a response to God in the midst of life (5 minutes).

- **Deepening our prayer life means learning to live prayerfully, to work worshipfully, and to walk in God's will wherever we are. This activity is an exercise in type 4 prayer—practicing openness of mind and heart to God at all times and among all people.**

- Two options are given for this particular exercise. Select the one that seems better for your group.

- Prepare by singing or saying the words of the hymn "Open My Eyes That I May See." Suggest that everyone claim a word or phrase as a breath prayer.

Option 1

Lead the group in an exercise of active prayer: seeing and responding to God in human life (20 minutes).

- Place on a table a number of drawings, photographs, or paintings (from magazines, art books, etc.) of real people and situations that convey human feeling and a variety of human conditions. Turn the pictures face down.

- Invite members to select a picture at random and accept it as their focus for prayerful reflection and listening to God.

- Ask the members to spend time gazing on their pictures and then to reflect in their journals on the following questions. Write the questions on newsprint or make a copy for each person.

    What do I see, hear, and feel? What is the human story behind the picture? (*Encounter life.*)

    What passage of scripture comes to mind, and what is the connection? (*Reflect on life in light of the Word.*)

    What does Christ see, hear, feel, and want to do? Write a conversation with Christ about this picture and what it represents for you both. (*Discern the presence of Christ.*)

    What is Christ saying to you (and to us) through this experience? (*Respond to God's call.*)

Gather the group together for sharing (15 minutes).

- Invite all to share their responses to this exercise: pictures and the feelings/stories they evoked, scriptures, and conversations with Christ.

- After all have shared, ask, **What is God saying to you or us through this experience?**

- Ask participants to be quiet where they are for five minutes, simply listening for God's call. **How is God speaking to you through this experience—questioning, blessing, challenging you? Write your impressions in your journal.** Then invite responses from the group.

Option 2

Lead the group in an experience of prayer in action (40 minutes).

- Plan ahead of time for the group to engage persons in an activity of ministry or outreach and to experience prayer in the context of that specific setting. Possibilities might include arranging for the group to visit a nearby nursing home or homeless shelter, assisting with children in the church's nursery or day-care center, making a few phone calls to some people who are unable to leave their homes, or taking a walk down a busy street or a ride on a city bus. Where possible, ask the group members to relate to the persons they encounter. You will know of many other possible activities of ministry or outreach.

- If you select this option, the group will need to extend the time period. A schedule might look like this: travel to the setting (10 minutes), spend time with the people (20 minutes), return to the meeting place (10 minutes). The group might find a space to reflect and pray at the ministry site itself and avoid returning to the meeting location.

- Engage in the ministry activity.

Gather the group for reflection and prayer (15 minutes).

- Lead the group in a conversation that invites personal and group reflection on their experience. Use the following questions. You may want to list the questions on newsprint or write the questions on newsprint after you have shared them with the group. Follow each question with a pause to allow for solitary reflection and even journaling before the participants speak. After the group has had a moment to absorb the question, ask the members to share their responses aloud. After the final question, give the group a little more time to listen prayerfully for the voice of Christ before sharing responses.

What did you see, hear, and feel? What is the human story that you saw and heard? (*Encounter life.*)

What passages of scripture come to mind, and what is the connection for you? (*Reflect on life in light of the Word.*)

Where was Christ? What does Christ see, hear, feel, and want to do? Where (about what) would you have liked to stop and have a conversation with Christ? (*Discern Christ's presence.*)

What is Christ saying to you (and to us) through this experience? How was Christ questioning, blessing, challenging you/us? (*Respond to God's call.*)

CLOSING (10 MINUTES)

Sing together one or two stanzas of "Take My Life and Let It Be."

Share. Give everyone an opportunity to voice briefly the sense of God's call received in this experience and the heart's response to that call.

Pray. Invite the group members to offer themselves to God in silent or spoken prayer in grateful response to the call they heard. Also invite prayers for the people the group encountered or persons whose needs were represented in the pictures used in the exercise.

Say or sing a benediction.

Psalms, the Prayer Book of the Bible

PREPARATION

Prepare yourself spiritually. Read the material for Week 5 of Part 3, do all the exercises, and keep a journal along with the participants. Spend time in prayer for your next group meeting and the ways that your group members are growing in their relationship with God.

Prepare materials and the room. Make sure you have hymnals or songbooks to accompany the songs you select for the "Opening" and "Closing." Arrange the room with a center table and candle.

Review the intent of this meeting: that participants grow in their appreciation for the use of psalms in prayer as individuals and in groups.

OPENING (**10 MINUTES**)

Welcome all participants by name as they enter.

Set the context.

This meeting is the fifth of six sessions for entering more deeply into the heart of Christ through prayer. This week we will expand our exploration of praying with psalms.

Join together in worship.

- **We light a candle to remember that Christ is in our midst as we gather in prayer.**

- Read Psalm 133 as a group in the following way: ask each person to read one verse or full line, in sequence around the circle. If necessary, read it through twice, continuing around the circle so that every voice is heard. Then read the psalm together in unison. Do this at a gentle pace with pauses so that it has a meditative quality. Invite the group to sense the richness of blessing conveyed by this psalm. (See page 114 for the NRSV translation of Psalm 133 and how it is broken into verses.)

- Sing "Blest Be the Tie That Binds" or "Companion Song."

Sharing Insights (45 minutes)

Ask the group members to identify where they have experienced God's presence in their lives this past week.

Invite sharing around the daily exercises. The Psalms tap into many strong emotions. Be prepared for a variety of reactions and outpourings from the daily exercises.

- Ask group members to identify which psalm or portion of a psalm (from the daily exercises) best reflects where they are in their lives and faith.

- Encourage members to share from their journals on a psalm exercise that tapped their depths or their creativity.

- Encourage them to be listeners: Practice listening for God in each person's reflections and story.

- As leader, model sharing by offering your response first (very briefly) or invite any participant who wishes to do so to begin the sharing.

- After all have shared, invite the group to identify any patterns or themes that surfaced.

Break (10 minutes)

Deeper Explorations (50 minutes)

Invite members to sit in triads to name their favorite psalm or a psalm that is speaking most deeply to them at this time, and why (10 minutes).

Lead the group through an experience of reflection and prayer guided by Psalm 23 (40 minutes total).

- Set a context: **Psalms express corporate prayer as well as personal prayer. They can lead us to pray in communion with God's people in every age who have prayed the same psalms. The Psalms enable an honest expression of ourselves in prayer to God. We are going to prepare for prayer with Psalm 23 by reflecting in a rather unusual way on what it means—through a reverse paraphrase.** (2 minutes)

- Invite each participant to write a reverse paraphrase of Psalm 23. Explain that a reverse paraphrase is writing lines that represent the opposite of what each verse or stanza means to you. For example, a person might reverse "The Lord is my shepherd" to say, "I have no God to guide me" or "There is no God." The value lies in helping us discover the real power of familiar words in a fresh way. Remind everyone that this is not a literary contest. There is no right or wrong way of doing it, only personal expression. (10 minutes)

- Share reverse paraphrases. Ask everyone to return to the circle and, if willing, to share his or her reverse paraphrase of Psalm 23. Following each sharing, you might say together, "The Lord is my shepherd, I shall not want." Be prepared for the despair that can be communicated through a reverse paraphrase of this psalm. Ask participants if they know or can imagine people who feel this way and experience life "having no hope and without God in the world" (Eph. 2:12). (15 minutes)

- Now invite the group to hear the grace in Psalm 23 afresh and to let the words of the psalm guide the group in a period of prayer. Explain that we will let the psalm guide our prayer time, one verse at a time. Following each verse, anyone may express prayers to God with positive paraphrases of the verse, petitions and intercessions, or other personal responses that the verse evokes. For example, Psalm 23:1 might inspire "O God, you are my shepherd and guide," "Lord, you have shepherded me even without my knowing it; I have ignored you most of my life," or "Shepherd of souls, find and guide my sister." Or the Spirit may move someone to sing a song to God. Begin with a moment of silent prayer, then read Psalm 23 verse by verse. Allow sufficient time for persons to soak in the meaning of the verse and offer their responses. (10 minutes)

- Conclude the time of prayer by having everyone read Psalm 23 in unison. (3 minutes)

CLOSING (5 MINUTES)

Take a moment to reflect on the experience.

Sing "The Lord's My Shepherd" (or any hymn/song based on Psalm 23) as a benediction.

Discuss the next meeting (Week 6 of Part 3). If you wish to close the meeting for Week 6 with the Lord's Supper, check with the group members to see if they could stay for an extra fifteen minutes. Also ask your pastor or another clergyperson to join and lead a brief Communion service.

Leader's Notes

PSALM 133 FOR READING IN SEQUENCE (NRSV)

How very good and pleasant it is
   when kindred live together in unity!
It is like the precious oil on the head,
   running down upon the beard,
on the beard of Aaron,
   running down over the collar of his robes.
It is like the dew of Hermon,
   which falls on the mountains of Zion.
For there the Lord ordained his blessing,
   life forevermore.

Part 3, Week 6
Exploring Contemplative Prayer

PREPARATION

Prepare yourself spiritually. Read the material for Week 6 of Part 3, do all the exercises, and keep a journal along with the participants. Spend time in prayer for openness to God's presence and guidance of the Spirit in your meeting time.

Prepare materials and the room. Secure some play dough (or modeling clay) and art materials for the closing process. Make sure you have a center table large enough to accommodate creative offerings. Select songs and have needed hymnals or song sheets. Obtain a small chime or bell, or a CD or audiocassette player and meditative musical selection, to call participants back from solitude. Arrange the room with a center table and candle. Make copies of the handout on page 119 for persons who may desire to use the reflection guide. Secure Communion elements if you intend to close with the Lord's Supper.

Review the intent of this meeting: that participants gain a deeper understanding of contemplative prayer and become more aware of the quality of their receptivity to God.

OPENING (10 MINUTES)

Welcome all participants personally as they enter.

Set the context.

This meeting is the last of six sessions on deepening our prayer, which draws us more fully into the heart of Christ. At this meeting we will continue to explore the practice of contemplative prayer, an aspect of prayer that has received little attention in many churches.

Join together in worship.

- Light a candle to represent Christ in our midst as we gather in prayer. Remember that the inner light of grace enables us to "see God," which is one way of understanding contemplation. Read Luke 1:38.

- Sing a hymn or song that expresses spiritual vision such as "Open My Eyes, That I May See"; "Be Thou My Vision"; or "Amazing Grace."

- Offer an opening prayer, or invite participants to offer one-sentence prayers of receptivity and praise.

SHARING INSIGHTS (45 MINUTES)

Ask the group members to identify where they have experienced God's presence in their lives this past week.

Invite sharing around the daily exercises.

- Ask group members to describe their experiences with the daily exercises, what went well, where they found sources of struggle, and what insights they gained.

- Then focus on Exercise 5, based on the story of Martha and Mary, and give each person an opportunity to share his or her experience, after first offering your own response.

- Encourage them to be listeners: Practice listening for God in each person's reflections and story.

- As leader, model sharing by offering your response first (very briefly) or invite any participant who wishes to do so to begin the sharing.

- After all have shared, invite the group to identify any patterns or themes that surfaced.

BREAK (10 MINUTES)

DEEPER EXPLORATIONS (45 MINUTES)

Introduce the theme of exploring contemplative prayer (5 minutes).

- Begin by prayerfully singing several rounds of "Spirit of the living God, fall afresh on me." Follow the singing with a few moments of silent receptivity to God's melting, molding presence.

- Explain that this song conveys the spirit of contemplative prayer. As the weekly reading points out, contemplative prayer is not the singing, the silence, a mysterious prayer method, or a special experience. Contemplative prayer is an intensified receptivity to the activity of God, whose love promises to purify and transform us in the likeness of Jesus Christ.

- The reading in the Participant's Book points out:

  "All Christians are called to contemplation."

  "In true contemplative prayer, one abides in mystery, open to being taken by God in love along a way one cannot know."

Set a context for a solitary prayer exercise with Luke 1:26-38 (5 minutes). One of the New Testament's finest portrayals of the spirit of contemplative prayer—of utter receptivity to God—is found in the story of the angel's visit to the young girl Mary whom God called to give birth to Jesus Christ. In the story we see the following, and you may want to present these points in your own words:

- In the Gospel of Luke, the life of Christ in the world begins when Mary resolves to say, "Here am I, the servant of the Lord; let it be with me according to your word."

- In uttering these words, Mary joins Moses (Exod. 3:4), Isaiah (6:8), Ananias (Acts 9:10), and others in placing herself totally at the disposal of God in receptivity and love.

- Mary has natural hesitations; she does not know what is in store for her. But in faith she ventures to trust God. She gives herself to God and to the promise of God's presence in her—the promise of Jesus Christ.

Begin the time of solitary prayer (20 minutes). Offer directions such as:

- **During these next few minutes, join Mary in being utterly receptive to God. Let Mary's response (or some portion of it) be your breath prayer: "Here am I, the servant of the Lord; let it be with me according to your word."**

- **Find a place where you can be present to God without interruption.**

- **Return when you hear the signal that it is time to gather** (such as playing music or ringing a bell).

Gather the group for individual reflection and creative expression (15 minutes).

- Invite group members to use the next fifteen minutes to shape a representation of what they feel is the promise of God's presence in them and how they feel about receiving it. Use words, play dough, or other art forms. If some would like simply to reflect, they may use the handout on page 119.

- Make available the handout sheet for reflection and the other materials.

- After fifteen minutes, ask people to bring what they have created to the closing worship.

CLOSING (10 MINUTES OR 25 MINUTES WITH COMMUNION)

Lead the group in singing, "Here I Am, Lord."

Invite everyone to share his or her creative expression or reflection and what each signifies. After each time of sharing, celebrate that person's offering by saying as a group, "Greetings, (name); the Lord is with you!"

Invite each person to place what she or he has made or written on the center table as an offering to God.

Conclude by singing a doxology or another familiar expression of praise and thanksgiving to God or with a simple service of Holy Communion, making the creative expressions an offering.

Reflection Sheet following Solitary Prayer Exercise
BASED ON LUKE 1:26-38

"Greetings, favored one! The Lord is with you. . . . And now, you will conceive in your womb and bear a son, and you will name him Jesus." *How are you noticing God's presence in you? What do you feel is the promise in God's presence or prompting?*

"But she was much perplexed . . . and pondered what sort of greeting this might be. . . . 'How can this be, since I am a virgin?'" *What hesitations, fears, questions prevent you from being utterly receptive to God's presence and promise?*

What assurance do you need?

"Here am I, the servant of the Lord; let it be with me according to your word."
When you say, "Here am I," what are you saying yes to or accepting? What are you saying no to or giving up?

What do you need in order to live your "Here am I" and give yourself in joy to the promise of Christ in you?

Responding to Our Call: The Work of Christ

Introductory Leader's Notes for Part 4

*P*art 4 presents vocation as a pathway of spiritual formation in the work of Christ. You have the privilege of guiding a process that will help people to identify God's call and gifts for ministry in their lives.

The test group leaders noted that Part 4 required more preparation time than previous parts. Schedule one to two hours per week of quality time to study and prepare for leading the sessions.

Before you begin preparing for Week 1 of Part 4, take time to survey the whole of Part 4. Pay attention to the flow of the five meetings and the various discovery experiences that you will facilitate in the "Deeper Explorations" and "Closings."

Scan the section called "Preparation" on the first page of all five weeks in Part 4 of the Leader's Guide for anything that may require you to plan ahead. For example, Week 2 calls for more materials than usual—play dough or modeling clay, candles, oil for anointing, and meditative music. Week 3 calls for basins and towels. Besides preparing for the weekly meeting, the Daily Exercises in Week 4 require you, along with everyone else, to write a "gift card" for each member of your group.

Anticipate the need to plan an additional session for completing Week 4, especially if you have more than eight persons in your group. The sharing of gifts is one of the highlights of the course for many participants and should not be cut short or rushed. Moreover, trying to complete the sharing of gifts by squeezing it into the next session compromises Week 5 and its focus on common ministry.

Some test groups felt that, because it was such a high point, the sharing of gifts would have been a fitting end for the entire course. Help your group to see that although the affirmation of gifts is a wonderfully clarifying experience, the work of discerning one's personal call and gifts is not an end in itself and is not complete apart from attention to the common call and ministry of the body of Christ. This is the theme of Week 5 and the basis for Part 5 on spiritual guidance.

May God be with you as you guide the group toward becoming companions in ministry.

Part 4, Week 1
Radical Availability

Prepare yourself spiritually. Read the material for Week 1 of Part 4, do all the exercises, and keep a journal along with the participants. Pray for each participant and for your group meeting.

Prepare materials and the room. Select songs or hymns for this session. Make sure you have appropriate hymnals or songbooks. Have a copy of the handout on the burning bush (page 127) for each participant. Be sure you have sufficient space for triad sharing in relative privacy. Arrange the chairs around a center table and candle.

Review the intent of this meeting: that participants notice the nature of God's call to them personally and that they become more aware of the character of their response.

OPENING (10 MINUTES)

Welcome all participants personally as they enter.

Set the context.

This is the first of five sessions inviting us to pay closer attention to God's call and claim on our lives and the ways in which we are or are not responding. This week we focus on God's "first call," the call that grounds every particular expression of Christian vocation.

Join together in worship.

- Light a candle to acknowledge the true spiritual presence of Christ in our midst, who illumines and enlivens our sense of call throughout our lives.

- Read the following paraphrase of the Great Commandment:

    Love the Lord your God with all your passion and prayer and muscle and intelligence and . . . love your neighbor as well as you do yourself.[1]

Invite a few moments of quiet reflection on how, this past week, participants have practiced or experienced loving God and neighbor with all their passion, prayer, muscle, and intelligence.

- Ask each person to share the one word that best expresses where he or she feels the love for God or neighbor is strongest right now: through passion, prayer, muscle, or intelligence.

- Sing a hymn or song that celebrates God's call and our desire to follow, such as "Jesus Calls Us O'er the Tumult"; "I Want to Walk as a Child of the Light"; "The Voice of God Is Calling"; "Tú Has Venido a la Orilla" ("Lord, You Have Come to the Lakeshore"); "Lord, I Want to Be a Christian"; "Here I Am, Lord"; "Take My Life, and Let It Be Consecrated"; or "The Summons."

SHARING INSIGHTS (45 MINUTES)

Ask the group members to identify where they have experienced God's presence in their lives this past week.

Invite sharing around the daily exercises.

- Give participants a moment to look over their journals and identify what spoke most deeply to them. You might begin by looking at Exercises 1 and 3.

- Encourage them to be listeners: Practice listening for God in each person's reflections and story.

- As leader, model sharing by offering your response first (very briefly) or invite any participant who wishes to do so to begin the sharing.

- Ask people to share their responses to one or more of the daily exercises.

- After all have shared, invite the group to identify any patterns or themes that surfaced.

BREAK (10 MINUTES)

DEEPER EXPLORATIONS (45 MINUTES)

Introduce the theme of learning radical availability to God (2 minutes).

- Where are you hearing God's call? What are you hearing God calling you to be and do? That's what we want to focus on as we continue our session. There are two sides to God's call in the Bible and in our lives.

- God calls us to give our all, to be God's people always.

- But God calls us to do so in particular ways here and now: to take up a task, assume a responsibility, or devote our lives to meeting a real need in the service of Christ. This is how we align our lives with God's will in the world.

- The story of Moses' call in Exodus 3–4 illustrates both sides of the call. Listening carefully to this story can help us refocus on where we are hearing God's call in our lives.

Set the context for the Burning Bush Exercise (8 minutes).

- Read Exodus 3:1-14 and Exodus 4:1, 10.

- Invite participants, as you read, to pay attention to the words or images that speak to them most vividly and then to name them briefly. What does the story mirror about the nature of a call or about discovering one's calling? (For example, an authentic call holds your attention, is persistent over time, seems to call to you by name, may seem impossible, sets your compassion on fire, requires dependence on God, conveys God's assurance, calls you beyond yourself, etc.)

- Then notice that the story of Moses' call reflects at least two movements in discovering *our* call:

First, the scripture reading reminds us to pay attention to the "burning bushes" that illumine the way and call us forward. We do this by noticing people, situations, and human needs that call us to turn aside and look—that give us a glimpse of God's purpose at work among us and the purpose for which God is empowering us to live. Burning bushes may be outside us, but they reflect something of God's presence, promise, and power at work in us.

Second, just as Moses did, we name our human fears and reservations about accepting God's call and can receive God's assurance. Fears always accompany an awareness of God's calling because God calls us to go beyond where we already are. But a sense of God's assurance and empowerment also accompanies a genuine awareness of God's call.

- Hand out the reflection sheet on Exodus 3–4, and invite each participant to spend fifteen minutes in solitary reflection using the handout.

Permit solitary reflection on Exodus 3:1-14; 4:1, 10 (10 minutes).

Listen in triads to God's call and assurance (25 minutes).

- Call everyone together, then form triads, and explain the process.

- Ask persons within the triads to take turns sharing directly from their reflection sheet on the two questions in the Burning Bush Exercise. The triads will give each person eight minutes to share as the other two listen and respond appropriately.

- As a person shares about the first question (burning bushes and sense of call), the two listeners can ask for clarification if necessary by gently and respectfully asking, "What did you see and hear?" When the person has finished sharing, the listeners take a minute to reflect the essence of what they heard. As the person shares from question #2 about his or her fears, the listeners respond together (as the Lord responded to Moses) with the words, "God says, 'I will be with you.'"

CLOSING (10 MINUTES)

Gather and bring closure to the experience by briefly naming insights from the session:

What you saw and heard anew related to your call.

How you experienced God's repeated assurance, "I will be with you."

Sing a song of assurance such as "Blessed Assurance," "Amazing Grace," or "Trust and Obey."

Close by offering this psalm portion as a prayer:

> O Most High,
> when I am afraid, I put my trust in you.
> In God, whose word I praise,
>   in God I trust; I am not afraid. . . .
>   This I know, that God is for me.
> In God, whose word I praise . . .
> in God I trust; I am not afraid.
>   (from Psalm 56)

Solitary Reflection on the Burning Bush
Exodus 3:1-14; 4:1, 10

"I must turn aside and look at this great sight."

Spend a few minutes turning aside to look at "burning bushes" in your life. Recall one to three luminous moments, penetrating insights, persistent concerns, or compelling encounters with human need that continue to speak to you of your calling in Christ. What is the common theme that you see or calling that you hear?

"Who am I that I should go to Pharaoh?"

What are your fears about heeding the call that you hear? In the space below, list your "Who am I . . . ?" feelings: reservations, objections, feelings of inadequacies, doubts, or obstacles.

Part 4, Week 2
Living Reliance

PREPARATION

Prepare yourself spiritually. Read the material for Week 2 of Part 4, do all the exercises, and keep a journal along with the participants. Pray for each participant and for your leadership, that you may be open to the guidance of the Holy Spirit.

Prepare materials and the room. Select songs or hymns for this session. Make sure you have appropriate hymnals and songbooks. Gather materials for the "Deeper Explorations" and "Closing": a small votive or tea candle for each person, matches, a small carton of play dough for each person or a significant quantity of modeling clay, and a plate and oil for the worship table. If you decide to play background music during the clay modeling time, select an audiocassette or CD and have a music player available. Arrange chairs around a center table and candle. Please notice that the "Sharing Insights" time has been shortened to thirty-five minutes to allow a longer time for the "Deeper Explorations" and "Closing."

Review the intent of this meeting: that participants gain a deeper desire and willingness to live in full reliance on Christ.

OPENING (10 MINUTES)

Welcome all participants personally as they enter.

Set the context.

This is the second of five sessions on God's call and our response. This week we focus on the theme of living reliance and what it means for us personally and together.

Join together in worship.

- Light a candle to celebrate the presence of Christ, the Living Vine into whom we are grafted by our baptism. As we abide in Christ, we have light to share with others.

- Invite participants to hold up the image of the vine and branches that they drew for Exercise 1. Place as many of them as possible on or around the center table. Hold hands or link arms around the table as a sign of union in the Vine. Suggest that the group look on the light of the Christ candle and meditate for a minute on the image of each person around the circle being a branch connected to the living vine of Christ, therefore connected deeply to one another. Read John 15:5.

- Sing a stanza or two of a hymn or song celebrating unity in Christ, such as: "One Bread, One Body"; "Blest Be the Tie That Binds"; or "We Are One in the Spirit."

SHARING INSIGHTS (35 MINUTES)

Ask the group members to identify where they have experienced God's presence in their lives this past week.

Invite sharing around the daily exercises.

- Give participants a moment to look over their journals and identify what spoke most deeply to them. You might want to begin with Exercises 2 and 5. Be sensitive that it may be difficult for persons to talk about their weaknesses and/or limitations. Be open to the Spirit's leading.

- Encourage them to be listeners: Practice listening for God in each person's reflections and story.

- As leader, model sharing by offering your response first (very briefly) or invite any participant who wishes to do so to begin the sharing.

- After all have shared, invite the group to identify any patterns or themes that surfaced.

BREAK (10 MINUTES)

DEEPER EXPLORATIONS (50 MINUTES)

Introduce the theme—learning to rely on the strength of Christ working through our weakness (10 minutes).

- Last week, we discussed how responding to God's call to be radically available is not an abstraction or something only special people do. This call involves two dimensions: making ourselves completely available ("Here am I") and paying attention to specific burning bushes where God may be sending us to live, to love, and to serve ("Send me").

- This week's reading reminds us that the quality of our response to God's call may depend more on how Christ works in and through our weakness than on how much we can do for Christ through our strengths. We want to rely on our strength of character, our skills, our talents, and so forth for doing God's work. But the way of the cross invites us to see that God may work more powerfully in and through our weakness.

- Through honest acceptance and offering to God of who we are in our weakness, we learn that we can rely on Christ to work in and through us. We are relieved of the illusion that we have to rely entirely on ourselves and our strength of character or skill to do all God wants.

- Read the following selection:

Our affluent culture expects that there is a way to fix almost anything that is broken—broken bodies, broken hearts, broken possessions. It is difficult for many of us to see brokenness as a part of life.

Within the tradition of the Native American Medicine Wheel, life is seen as a circle, as a whole, incorporating birth and death, the peaceful dawn and the thundering storms, wholeness and brokenness. From the northern direction of the Medicine Wheel come the storms of life. It is the storms that bring us courage and wisdom and compassion. Our lives would not be whole without the storms.

Richard Rohr says, "The place of the wound is the place of the healing. The place of the break is the place of the greatest strength." Our Christian faith affirms this—that Christ's wounds are the place where God's healing touches each of us.

Perhaps the task for us today is to begin to see the gifts of our broken places. To find the opportunities to believe in the mystery of Christ's death, "to put our finger in the wound of Christ, our own wounds, and the wounds of each other" (Richard Rohr, *Breathing under Water*, audiocassette).[1]

Lead a brief discussion of 2 Corinthians 4:6-12 (10 minutes).

- Read the passage, inviting people to visualize what Paul is saying.

- Ask people to share their understanding of the meaning of this passage. **What are the characteristics and purpose of clay jars? What does the image of clay jars or pots say about us? about God?**

- Be prepared to help people deepen their understanding of this image, if necessary. **Paul presents here a rich, even humorous, image of our lives as clay jars that are cracked, imperfect, and weakened by difficulties we encounter as we seek to respond to God's call. The purpose of clay pots is to carry something and not to be perfect for their own sake. Paul emphasizes that the clay pots are imperfect and cracked by the hard knocks of life. Their very imperfection allows the extraordinary power of God to shine through! Because we are cracked pots, "the life of Jesus may . . . be made visible in our bodies."**

Lead the group in a meditation on the treasure in clay jars (15 minutes).

- Give each person a ball of play dough or modeling clay and a votive or tea candle. Ask everyone to spend some time working with the dough and shaping a "clay jar" that represents his or her actual life. Put in it the cracks and crevices, imperfections and weaknesses, deep impressions and experiences that make you who you are before God.

- Assure all group members, in the spirit of the passage, that they need not make a perfect pot. What God wants is a clay jar that allows the light of Christ to shine through it and from it. The one requirement is that they shape the jar so the candle can fit inside.

- Encourage them to let the Spirit lead as they shape their clay jar, making space for God in their hearts with the prayerful affirmation, "We have this treasure in clay jars. . . ."

- You may want to play some quiet music as background for this exercise.

- Conclude the creative time by asking participants to take a final moment in silence to contemplate what they have created, what it mirrors about their lives and the light within, and what they would like to share about their clay pot with the rest of the group.

Gather together (15 minutes).

- Invite the participants to set their clay pot on the table with the votive or tea candle inside and light the candle.

- Go around the circle inviting everyone to share his or her precious, uniquely imperfect clay jar. Ask each to share briefly (*1 minute each*) about some of its features that either allow light to shine through or block the light.

- After each person's sharing, you might lead the group in saying an affirmation such as "___*(Name)*___, arise, shine, for your light has come, and the glory of the Lord has risen upon you" (Isaiah 60:1). [*Print words on newsprint or on a card for each person.*]

CLOSING (15 MINUTES)

Invite all to gather around the worship table with their clay jars and candles in hand.

- Place on the table a plate with a small amount of oil.

- Ask someone to read 2 Corinthians 4:6-12 again.

- Offer this quote from Henri Nouwen's book *The Wounded Healer*:

    A Christian community is therefore a healing community not because wounds are cured and pains alleviated, but because wounds and pains become openings or occasions for a new vision.[2]

- Acknowledge that the exercise with the Second Corinthians passage may have surfaced an area of weakness or a wound that yearns to become an opening or occasion for God's light to shine through. Invite group members to participate in a healing service where those wounds can be made available to God's redeeming grace. Point out that on the table there is a plate with oil—a symbol of Christ's healing, anointing, empowering presence.

- Give everyone an opportunity to identify an area of personal need by speaking aloud a single word or phrase. As each person speaks, let another member of the group (whoever feels led to do so) step forward to touch a finger to the oil and then to anoint the person's forehead on behalf of the body of Christ.

- Lead the group, together with the anointer, in speaking a blessing for each person who has named an area in need of healing. Use these words: "My grace is sufficient for you, for power is made perfect in weakness" (2 Cor. 12:9). (This phrase could be written on newsprint in large letters or copied onto cards for each person to hold.) Make it clear that group members have permission not to speak, if they so desire.

- Sing "Let Your Light Shine," "This Little Light of Mine," "The Lord Is My Light" (Taizé), "Within Our Darkest Night" (Taizé), or another appropriate song.

Close by offering a brief benediction.

Leader's Notes

*N*ext week's meeting includes a foot-washing service. If you plan to use this material, you may want to alert the group members to the nature of the service and invite them to wear sandals or easily removable shoes. Let women in the group know that it is fine to keep hose on for a foot washing, since they dry quickly.

Bearing the Fruit of the Vine

PREPARATION

Prepare yourself spiritually. Read the material for Week 3 of Part 4, do all the exercises, and keep a journal along with the participants. Pray that God will prepare you and each participant to receive the greatest benefit from your group meeting.

Prepare materials and the room. Select songs and gather hymnals/songbooks. Arrange the room and have copies of the handout on John 13:1-17 (pages 141–42). Also have prepared a pitcher of water, two basins, and two towels for the foot-washing service. It would help to play an audiocassette of meditative music during this part of the session, and candles are a nice touch. During the "Closing," you will distribute a small hand towel or washcloth to each person, so purchase or collect a sufficient number for the group. Set the chairs in a circle with a center table and candle.

Review the intent of this meeting: that group members will grow in their understanding of what it means to be fruitful as Christ's disciples and what it means to live as servants, following the model of their Lord.

OPENING (10 MINUTES)

Welcome all participants personally as they enter.

Set the context.

This meeting is the third of five sessions on God's call and our response in Christian vocation. This week we are exploring further the image of the vine and the branches in relation to the theme of fruitfulness.

Join together in worship.

- Light a candle to celebrate the presence of Christ our Lord, whose spirit is fertile in love and who wants to bestow this fruitfulness upon us.

- Read Ephesians 3:16-19. Invite the group to reflect on the image of being "rooted and grounded in love," then to imagine what it would be like to be "filled with all the fullness of God."

- After a few minutes, invite participants to share a word, insight, or image that has spoken to them.

- Sing a few stanzas of a familiar song or hymn such as "Breathe on Me, Breath of God"; "Spirit of the Living God"; "Sanctuary"; or "Alleluia."

SHARING INSIGHTS (45 MINUTES)

Ask the group members to identify where they have experienced God's presence in their lives this past week.

Invite sharing around the daily exercises.

- Give participants a moment to look over their journals and identify what seemed to be most challenging to them in the daily exercises. Pay special attention to allowing time for persons to share their reflections on Exercise 4. This is a beginning point for participants to begin to look not only at their own lives, but also at the whole congregation.

- Encourage them to be listeners: Practice listening for God in each person's reflections and story.

- As leader, model sharing by offering your response first (very briefly) or invite any participant who wishes to do so to begin the sharing.

- After all have shared, invite the group to identify any patterns or themes that surfaced.

BREAK (10 MINUTES)

Prepare all the material for the foot-washing service (see guidelines on page 139).

DEEPER EXPLORATIONS (45 MINUTES)

Introduce the theme (2 minutes).

- The material in the Participant's Book for Weeks 2 and 3 of Part 4 focuses on the image of a vine and its branches in John 15 as a way of understanding what it means to live in reliance on Christ and to bear the fruit of the vine.

- Another biblical image for what it means to bear the fruit of the vine and live in reliance on Christ is John 13:1-17—the story of Jesus taking up the towel of a servant and washing his disciples' feet.

Read aloud John 13:1-17 (3 minutes), and allow for a time of solitary reflection (10 minutes).

- As you read the passage the first time, ask the group to pay attention to what they see, hear, smell, and feel. Suggest that they listen for words and phrases that catch their attention, words that they hear as though for the first time, or words that make them "turn aside and look."

- Invite participants to share in a word or phrase what they see or hear.

- During the second reading, suggest that each person pay attention to what it says or suggests about being fruitful or unfruitful, and about the source of either. Then distribute reflection sheets (pages 141–42) to all participants and ask them to take about ten minutes to reflect in solitude.

Invite the group to share any central insights from their reflection on John 13:1-17 (10 minutes).

(See the Leader's Notes on page 140 for additional background information.)

Introduce and lead the service of foot washing (15 minutes).

- Ask everyone to take a chair in the circle. Introduce foot washing by pointing out that Jesus says three times they should "wash one another's feet." This is the Gospel writer's way of emphasizing the importance of the point. Jesus also gives an actual demonstration. Jesus is urging us to put this model of servanthood into practice.

- Select another person to begin the foot washing with you. Consider playing quiet, meditative music during the foot washing.

- Working with one basin and towel each, you and the person you have selected will lead off by getting up from your seats and unhurriedly washing the feet of the persons sitting next to you. You first take off their shoes, and then, with one foot and then the other over the bowl, ladle the foot with warm water. Or, pour the water from a pitcher over the feet into the basin. Towel off the feet and pass the towel to the one sitting. Go back to your own chairs. This continues until everyone has washed someone else's feet and has been washed by someone.[1]

Let the group have a brief time to talk about this experience at the completion of the service (5 minutes).

* Read John 13:12: "After he had washed their feet, had put on his robe, and had returned to the table, he said to them, 'Do you know what I have done to you?'"

* Ask the group to reflect on the following questions: **What has Jesus done to us? What did the foot-washing experience do to us? What does this experience, together with the story, tell us about bearing the fruit of Christ's life into the world? How has God touched us or spoken to us?**

CLOSING (10 MINUTES)

Announce to the group the special nature of the daily exercises for this next week. Be sure all members understand that they will be writing cards for one another and that they will be reading the cards during the next group meeting. A decision concerning whether your group will require more than one session to complete the sharing of gifts cards needs to be clear by now. If two meetings are needed, divide the group so members know to whom they write cards each week. If the group numbers more than eight persons, you will not have adequate time with one session. (Please see Introductory Leader's Notes for Part 4.)

Read John 13:14-17.

Distribute a hand towel or washcloth to each participant.

* Wrap a towel around your waist. Then give each person a towel or washcloth. Explain that the towel you are giving to each symbolizes the fruitful life Jesus has given us and that he wants to reproduce in us.

* Invite them to a few moments of silence to consider what it means to receive and to go about their daily lives at home and work with the towel of Christ's servanthood tied around their waists. Encourage them to wear the towel this week, either literally or figuratively, as a reminder of who they are and of their readiness to respond to the call of the Master.

Pray an appropriate prayer such as:

> Loving God, in Jesus Christ you showed us the greatest of humility. Give us grace now to serve one another in simplicity of heart, and so enter into the fellowship of his service. Amen.

Conclude with a hymn or song such as: "Jesu, Jesu, Fill Us with Your Love"; "O Master, Let Me Walk with Thee"; or "Lord, Speak to Me, That I May Speak."

Guidelines for a Foot Washing

Gather the equipment you need for a foot washing ahead of time. Consider asking a group member to assist in gathering the items.

The equipment you need includes two basins (or bowls) and two towels. Remember to also bring a pitcher of water.

Consider featuring a bowl, towel, and pitcher as a centerpiece on a table or altar.

During the break, have someone help you prepare the bowls and towels and put them in place. Pour some water into each bowl but do not fill it.

Before the foot washing begins, encourage women who are anxious about their hose to keep them on rather than delay the activity. The hose dry quickly after being towel dried.

Set the tone for the experience by being positive and inviting. Anticipate other obstacles or potential concerns among your group members, and be prepared to address or accommodate them.

Give persons permission not to participate, especially if kneeling to wash another's feet is a problem for them.

Leader's Notes

BACKGROUND ON FOOT WASHING IN JOHN 13:1-17

Foot washing was common in Jesus' day. It was done for hygiene and for hospitality.

Upon entering a home, people washed their own feet to remove dust or caked mud. Wealthy hosts had servants wash the feet of honored guests as a way of welcoming them.

What was not common was for a host to wash guests' feet personally and, in so doing, to take on the humble role meant for a servant.

In this story, Jesus' concern was not so much for physical hygiene; he washed the disciples' feet halfway through the meal, not as they entered the house or approached the table. So Jesus' unexpected action is one of hospitality.

Listen to Jesus' response to Peter's objection: "Unless I wash you, you have no share with me." Jesus yearns for Peter and the other disciples to share his life. He welcomes his friends into his "home" and invites them by example to share in the way that life in the Father's house is to be lived—as servants to one another in love.

Gail R. O'Day writes in the *New Interpreter's Bible* (vol. IX, 727–28), "The foot washing reveals Jesus' unfettered love for the disciples, and it is this love that holds the promise of new life for the disciples. The call for the disciples is to allow themselves to be ministered to in this way, to accept Jesus' gesture of love fully. . . . Jesus does not simply issue a general call for service; he issues a call to give as he gives, to love as he loves."

Solitary Reflection on John 13:1-17

"And during supper Jesus, knowing that the Father had given all things into his hands, and that he had come from God and was going to God, got up from the table."

Meditate on what these verses say Jesus knows and how that knowing relates to his capacity to be available to God. What do you know in your heart that enables you to be available to God to the extent that you are?

"And during supper Jesus . . . got up from the table, took off his outer robe, and tied a towel around himself."

Meditate on Jesus' removing his outer robe. What did Jesus have to take off in order to take up the towel? What "outer robe" do you have to take off, figuratively speaking, in order to take up the towel in the spirit of Jesus?

"Then he poured water into a basin and began to wash the disciples' feet and to wipe them with the towel that was tied around him."

Contemplate how low Jesus stooped to show God's love for the disciples, for us. What current situation is challenging you to stoop low in love? How low are you willing to stoop for Christ's sake?

"He came to Simon Peter, who said to him, 'Lord, are you going to wash my feet? . . . You will never wash my feet.' Jesus answered, 'Unless I wash you, you have no share with me.'"

What are your reservations about sharing Christ's life more fully than you do now? What are your fears? What are your hopes?

"Not all of you are clean."

Jesus knew Judas was going to betray him, and yet he washed his feet anyway. Whose feet would you find difficult, if not impossible, to wash?

"So if I, your Lord and Teacher, have washed your feet, you also ought to wash one another's feet."

If you were daily wearing the symbolic towel of servanthood around your waist, what would you be paying attention to that you now miss? What particular relationships would be affected the most? How?

Part 4, Week 4
Gifts of the Spirit

PREPARATION

Prepare yourself spiritually. Read the material for Week 4 of Part 4, do all the exercises, and keep a journal along with the participants. Spend time in prayer seeking God's guidance for the group meeting, and pray for each participant.

Prepare materials and the room. Choose your songs and have available appropriate hymnals or songbooks. Set chairs in a circle with a center table and candle.

Review the intent of this meeting: 1) that participants gain experience in speaking the truth concerning others' gifts in a spirit of honesty, affirmation, and love; and 2) that they begin to accept and receive affirmation for their own gifts in a spirit of gratitude and humble confidence.

Please note that the "Sharing Insights" time has been reduced to fifteen minutes in order to allow more time for the naming of gifts in "Deeper Explorations."

OPENING (10 MINUTES)

Welcome all participants personally as they enter.

Set a context.

This is our fourth session on God's call and our response. This week we focus on discernment of one another's spiritual gifts as we consider our deeper vocation in the life of faith.

Join together in worship.

- Light a candle to recall the illumination of mind and heart that comes when God reveals the gifts that the Holy Spirit gives to each believer for building up the body of Christ. Read 1 Corinthians 12:4-6.

- Sing a song or hymn that celebrates the varied gifts of the faith community such as "Many Gifts, One Spirit"; "The Gift of Love"; "We All Are One in Mission"; "We Are Your People"; or "We Give Thee But Thine Own."

- Invite brief prayers from the group for gifts of discernment and clarity in this time.

SHARING INSIGHTS (15 MINUTES)

Invite a very brief sharing around the daily exercises. Give the group members an opportunity to share briefly how they experienced the process of naming and affirming the gifts of other group members.

BREAK (10 MINUTES)

DEEPER EXPLORATIONS (75 MINUTES)

Devote the entire time to the process of affirming gifts that we see in one another.

- Prayerfully focus the group's attention on one person at a time.

- Go around the circle, having members of the group use what they wrote on their gift cards to name and affirm the gifts they see in the person-in-focus. After each person shares the list on the card, he or she should give the card to the person-in-focus. When the whole group has completed the process of affirming gifts for one member, give that person an opportunity to respond briefly (gratitude, insights, confirmations). Continue until every member of the group has been both on the receiving and the giving ends of this process.

- Consider the total time available, and establish clear expectations about the number of minutes available for each person to receive affirmations and to respond to them. Encourage those who are naming gifts to stay close to their notes so as to avoid unnecessary elaboration. Also encourage those receiving affirmation to keep their responses brief. They will have an opportunity next week to say more about their responses.

CLOSING (10 MINUTES)

Allow a few minutes of silence for participants to absorb what has been offered and received.

Invite spontaneous prayers of thanksgiving and supplication, as people feel moved.

Read or sing the hymn text, "Whom Shall I Send?," by Fred Pratt Green if your hymnal includes this hymn. If not, sing "We Give Thee But Thine Own," inviting the group to think in terms of the gifts identified this day.

Conclude with a spoken or sung benediction.

Part 4, Week 5
The Body of Christ Given for the World

PREPARATION

Prepare yourself spiritually. Read the material for Week 5 of Part 4, do all the exercises, and keep a journal along with the participants. Spend time in prayer for an openness to God's presence and guidance of the Spirit in your meeting time.

Prepare materials and the room. Select songs and gather needed hymnals or songbooks. Arrange the room with a center table and candle. If you plan to close with the Lord's Supper, secure the Communion elements. If you plan to close with a Love Feast, contact your minister for suggestions about this type of worship service.

Review the intent of this meeting: that participants continue to name and internalize their own gifts and call and that they begin to think corporately, exploring the gifts and call of this group and/or of their congregation.

OPENING (10 MINUTES)

Welcome all participants personally as they enter.

Set the context.

This is the final session on God's call and the gifts God gives us to fulfill our vocation in response to that call. This week we will focus on the spiritual gifts we feel ready to claim personally and begin to explore any possible sense of calling as a group within the church.

Join together in worship.

- Light a candle to proclaim and celebrate the presence of the Holy Spirit, who bestows God's gifts on all believers for strengthening the body of Christ to continue his ministry in the world. Read Philippians 1:6.

- Sing a song or hymn that calls us to minister in Jesus' name through the use of God's gifts. Suggestions include the following: "Awake, Awake to Love and Work"; "In God's Image"; "Lord, You Give the Great Commission"; "Come, Labor On"; or "How Clear Is Our Vocation, Lord."

- Offer an opening prayer, or invite brief sentences of prayer from the group.

SHARING INSIGHTS (45 MINUTES)

Ask the group members to identify where they have experienced God's presence in their lives this past week.

Invite sharing around the daily exercises.

- After giving time for all the group members to look over their journals, ask them to share first in response to Exercise 1—the naming of individual gifts and a sense of call they claim for themselves. Then turn attention to Exercises 2 and 5 and people's insight about God's call in and to your church. As leader, model sharing by offering your response first very briefly.

- Encourage them to be listeners: Practice listening for God in each person's reflections and story.

- After all have shared, invite the group to identify any patterns or themes that surfaced.

BREAK (10 MINUTES)

DEEPER EXPLORATIONS (45 MINUTES)

Introduce the theme of exploring God's call to our small group as a part of the body of Christ (5 minutes).

- We have listened for God's call as individuals within the group; now let's listen for God's call as a group within the church.

- Every group in the church, just like every cell in the body, has a call and a mission. We know that part of the call of this group is to be companions in Christ through sharing this formative experience. Do we discern another level of God's call to us as a group—maybe for the sake of the church, or our community, or some particular "burning bush" that we all see? We have an opportunity now to listen for where God might be calling us to move farther in this journey together. No one is expected to commit to anything except to being available to God's will.

Learn the lesson of the loaves—Mark 6:30-44 (40 minutes).

- The following exercise is a form of group *lectio* with scripture. The starting place of this story is similar to where we are now. The disciples are "on retreat" and get called out unexpectedly. Let's listen for God's word to see if we too are being called out.

- The scripture passage will be read three times, followed by a period of silent or directed reflection, then time for group sharing. [Pages 150–52 will give you, as leader, detailed directions for the entire group *lectio*.] You will need to have your journals to capture any images or ideas that come to mind during the second reading.

- In the course of the readings, silence, and sharing, listen with your hearts for God's call beneath the surface to the whole group. Remember: God may speak to us through the least likely, most unexpected thought or voice or insight. In the sharing times we will aim to be succinct and prayerful.

CLOSING (15 MINUTES)

Offer a brief service of Holy Communion beginning with prayers of the people and "The Great Thanksgiving." Allow the readings and meditation with Mark 6:30-46 to serve as the proclamation of the Word and response to the Word. If no ordained pastor is present or available to lead a Communion service, use a simplified Agape or Love Feast service instead.

Sing any Communion hymn or one of those listed in the "Opening" for this session.

Leader's Outline of Exercise on Mark 6:30-44
Learning the Lesson of the Loaves

First reading and brief sharing (5 minutes): Ask the group members to listen to the scripture for the overall sense of the story. Invite them to notice images, words, and phrases that catch their attention, linger in the mind, or words that they seem to be hearing for the first time. After the reading, the group members can share briefly what they noticed from this first reading.

Second reading and directed reflection (25 minutes): Invite participants to listen to the story as it is read verse by verse (see below). Allow the following questions to guide their reflections, and ask them to silently jot down insights in their journals after each reflection. Tell them that you will stop after each verse and set of reflection questions so that the group can briefly share their responses. Keep the meditation flowing; avoid getting stuck in discussions or differing interpretations.

1. "The apostles gathered around Jesus, and told him all that they had done and taught. He said to them, 'Come away to a deserted place all by yourselves and rest for a while.' For many were coming and going, and they had no leisure even to eat. And they went away in the boat to a deserted place by themselves."

In what ways have our meetings been for you/for us a gathering around Jesus, a deserted place all by ourselves, a time to rest for a while, apart from the comings and goings of our busy lives? (Pause for silent reflection.)

Invite succinct responses from persons without commentary or discussion.

2. "Now many saw them going and recognized them, and they hurried there on foot from all the towns and arrived ahead of them."

Who are these people in the story, and what are they looking for? (Pause for silent reflection.)

Who are the people in our community who are searching and hungering, and what are they looking for? (Pause for silent reflection.)

Invite succinct responses without commentary or discussion.

3. "As he went ashore, he saw a great crowd; and he had compassion for them, because they were like sheep without a shepherd; and he began to teach them many things."

What did Jesus see in the people that moved him? (Pause for silent reflection.)

What do you see in the people in your community that moves you to compassion? (Pause for silent reflection.)

Invite succinct responses without commentary or discussion.

4. "When it grew late his disciples came to him and said, 'This is a deserted place, and the hour is now very late; send them away so that they may go into the surrounding country and villages and buy something for themselves to eat.'"

How did the disciples want to respond to the need they saw? (Pause for silent reflection.)

How do you, how does your church, respond to hungers or needs that you see? (Pause for silent reflection.)

Invite succinct responses without commentary or discussion.

5. "But he answered them, 'You give them something to eat.'"

When you hear Jesus say, "You give them something to eat," what is your reaction? (Pause for silent reflection.)

Invite succinct responses without commentary or discussion.

6. "They said to him, 'Are we to go and buy two hundred denarii worth of bread, and give it to them to eat?' And he said to them, 'How many loaves have you? Go and see.' When they had found out, they said, 'Five [loaves], and two fish.'"

What assumptions shaped the disciples' view of the resources that were available to them and where they would find them? (Pause for silent reflection.)

What resources do you find are available for the need at hand? (Pause for silent reflection.)

Invite succinct responses without commentary or discussion.

7. "Then he ordered them to get all the people to sit down in groups on the green grass. So they sat down in groups of hundreds and of fifties. Taking the five loaves and the two fish, he looked up to heaven, and blessed and broke the loaves, and gave them to

his disciples to set before the people; and he divided the two fish among them all. And all ate and were filled; and they took up twelve baskets full of broken pieces and of the fish. Those who had eaten the loaves numbered five thousand men." (Matthew 14:21 adds, "besides women and children.")

What did Jesus have the disciples do with what meager resources they had? (Pause for silent reflection.)

What is Jesus calling us to do with the resources we have to help people find bread for the hungers of their hearts? (Pause for silent reflection.)

Invite succinct responses without commentary or discussion.

Third reading, silence, and sharing (10 minutes): Following the reading, allow one minute for silent awareness and listening to God's call in our hearts. Then invite the participants to speak out of the silence about what they are hearing.

Part 5

Exploring Spiritual Guidance: The Spirit of Christ

Introductory Leader's Notes for Part 5

*P*art 5 presents spiritual guidance as a pathway of spiritual formation in the spirit of Christ. Your role is to assist the group in exploring ways to become what God intends the church to be: a community of grace and guidance among those who are called to enter and grow fully into the mind, heart, and work of Christ.

As with Part 4, Part 5 may require more time for preparation. The material may be less familiar and thus require more study. So schedule one to two hours per week of quality time to study and prepare for leading the sessions.

Before you begin preparing for Week 1 of Part 5, take time to survey the whole of Part 5. Familiarize yourself with the flow of the five meetings and the various discovery experiences that you will facilitate in the "Deeper Explorations" and "Closings."

Scan the section called "Preparation" on the first page of all five weeks of the Leader's Guide for anything that may require you to plan ahead.

The "Deeper Explorations" in Week 2 calls for personal discernment of an issue in your life that can serve as a focus for the Clearness Committee group exercise. Identifying an appropriate issue or dilemma that you would be willing to share with the group may take some time. You will also need to identify and prepare another member of the group to serve as a facilitator for this particular process.

The "Deeper Explorations" in Week 4 calls for identification of a church concern or ministry dilemma that would be a workable focus for the exercise in corporate discernment. Give yourself time to think about it and to become familiar with the steps in the discernment process.

The "Deeper Explorations" in Week 5 is about the implications of this entire course for your church. Help the group see that the purpose of *Companions in Christ* is to enhance the spiritual life and ministry of the church as a community of grace and guidance for the Christian journey.

Begin now to schedule a time and place for the closing retreat. Look at page 183 for the preparations needed. After the closing retreat, take a little time to complete the evaluation found on page 239 in the Leader's Guide.

Please send your evaluation to *Companions in Christ*, Upper Room Ministries, P. O. Box 340004, Nashville, Tennessee 37203-0012, so we can continue to improve this small-group resource. Also feel free to contact us if you are seeking ideas and resources for follow-up programs or next steps as a group. The Participant's Book contains an annotated resource list with some suggestions that might be helpful as follow-up material for small groups or individual reading.

May God be with you as you guide the group toward becoming companions in Christ for your congregation.

Part 5, Week 1

How Do I Know God's Will for My Life?

PREPARATION

Prepare yourself spiritually. Read the material for Week 1 of Part 5, do all the exercises, and keep a journal along with the participants. Pray for each person in your group and for the group meeting.

Prepare materials and the room. Select songs or hymns for this session. Make sure that you have appropriate hymnals or songbooks. Have sufficient copies of the handout on the "Holy Listening Exercise" (pages 159–60). Bring a bell or chime to ring at the midpoint of the "Holy Listening Exercise." Arrange the chairs around a center table and candle.

Review the intent of the meeting: that participants gain clarity about the nature of spiritual guidance and have an opportunity to practice holy listening with one other person.

OPENING (10 MINUTES)

Welcome all participants personally as they enter.

Set a context.

This is our first meeting of five on the nature and practice of spiritual guidance. We are beginning this week with a focus on one-on-one guidance. In the next several weeks we will explore various expressions of corporate guidance in the church. All forms of spiritual guidance are expressions of the work of Christ in the world, through the action of the Holy Spirit. Let's reflect for a moment on the role of the Holy Spirit in our faith.

Join together in worship.

- Light the candle and read John 14:15-17. Invite a moment of silent reflection on how the Spirit is described in these few verses. Ask a few simple questions such as these: **When we hear the term *Advocate*, what word associations or images come to mind?**

(Invite a minute of sharing responses.) **What does "Spirit of truth" mean to you?** (Invite brief sharing of thoughts.) **Where does the passage say the Spirit will be found or known?** (Invite reflection on the extraordinary truth that the Spirit abides with us and in us.)

• Point out that this truth is the foundation of all spiritual guidance. If the Spirit did not graciously abide with us and in us, there would be no possibility that we could be vessels of God's guidance for one another.

• Sing a song that celebrates the vital presence of God's spirit in our faith journey such as "Spirit of the Living God"; "Breathe on Me, Breath of God"; "Spirit of God, Descend upon My Heart"; or "Spirit, Now Live in Me."

• Offer a brief prayer of thanksgiving and opening to the Spirit's work in our midst now.

SHARING INSIGHTS (45 MINUTES)

Ask the group members to identify where they have experienced God's presence in their lives this past week. Pay special attention to how each person responded to Exercise 5, the practice of examen.

Invite sharing around the daily exercises.

• As participants share around the daily exercises, focus on the nature of spiritual guidance that is illustrated in the scripture passages.

• As leader, model sharing by offering your response first (very briefly) or invite any participant who wishes to do so to begin the sharing.

• After all have shared, invite the group to identify any patterns or themes that surfaced.

BREAK (10 MINUTES)

DEEPER EXPLORATIONS (45 MINUTES)

Clarify an understanding of spiritual guidance as needed (10 minutes).

• On a sheet of newsprint or chalkboard, make three columns headed "Spiritual Guidance," "Counseling," and "Psychotherapy." (See Leader's Notes titled "Contrasts in Helping Relationships," page 161.)

- Then read the following definition of spiritual guidance from *The Art of Christian Listening* by Thomas N. Hart:

  The purpose of direction will be to sensitize people further to the presence and action of God in their lives, and to assist them to make a fuller and more appropriate response to it.[1]

- Invite group members to suggest ways that spiritual guidance, counseling, and therapy are alike and different, using this definition and material in the weekly reading.

Introduce the "Holy Listening Exercise" (5 minutes).

- The purpose of this exercise is to give everyone a chance to practice prayerful or holy listening. This is the heart of a spiritual-friendship relationship whether formal or informal, one-on-one, or in a group.

- Invite the group members to pair up for the exercise, preferably with someone they do not know too well.

- Give everyone the "Holy Listening Exercise" and "Review Questions" handouts. Explain the process to the group.

- Make sure participants understand that each person will have opportunity to be both a listener and a speaker. After the first eight minutes, they will take two minutes to reflect on the review questions on the handout. Then they will trade roles. At the end of each eight-minute session, they are to take two minutes to reflect quietly with the review questions on the handout. During the last five minutes they will compare their responses to the review questions

Practice holy listening in pairs (25 minutes).

- Ask pairs to find a space apart as quickly as possible and to make the most of the time.

- Help participants honor the time by ringing a bell or calling out the time after each eight-minute period and by reminding them to take two minutes to reflect on the review questions. Alert the participants at the close of the two minutes of reflection time to change roles.

- After the second listening session and evaluation, invite each pair to compare notes on their experiences for five minutes.

Gather as a group (5 minutes).

Finally, invite the pairs to join together as a total group and to share their experiences and learnings about holy listening.

CLOSING (10 MINUTES)

Light a candle and read Psalm 81:13, 16. Say a word or two about God's great yearning for us to listen and be attentive and the promise of being spiritually fed when we hear.

Invite silent reflection on what we have learned about holy listening with and from one another.

Invite a time of group prayer, to lift each person to God in thanksgiving and to celebrate the gift of God in each person as received during holy listening. When the prayer time is concluded, invite each person to be in prayer for the listening partner throughout the week and to remain open to any promptings of the Spirit.

Sing together a concluding benediction or one of the songs suggested in the "Opening."

Holy Listening Exercise

"Spiritual direction takes place when two people agree to give their full attention to what God is doing in one (or both) of their lives and seek to respond in faith."[2]

The purpose of this exercise is for each participant to practice holy listening in pairs.

AS THE SPEAKER

Receive your chance to speak and be heard as an opportunity to explore some aspect of your walk with God during the past week (or day). Remember that you and your friend meet in the company of God, who is the true guiding presence of this time together.

AS THE LISTENER

Practice listening with your heart as well as your head. Create a welcoming, accepting space for the other person to explore freely his or her journey in your presence and in the presence of God. Be natural, but be alert to any habits or anxious needs in you to analyze, judge, counsel, "fix," teach, or share your own experience. Try to limit your speech to gentle questions and honest words of encouragement.

Be inwardly prayerful as you listen, paying attention to the Spirit even as you listen to the holy mystery of the person before you.

When it seems appropriate and unintrusive, invite the other person to explore simple questions such as these:

- Where did you experience God's grace or presence in the midst of this?

- Do you sense God calling you to take a step forward in faith or love? Is there an invitation here to explore?

HOW TO BEGIN AND END THE CONVERSATION

- Decide who will be the first listener and begin with a moment of silent prayer.

- Converse for eight minutes; then pause for two minutes so that each person may respond to the review questions in silence.

- Trade roles and converse for eight minutes more; then pause again for personal review.

- Use the last five minutes to compare notes on your experiences and your responses to the review questions.

Review Questions

FOR THE LISTENER

a. When were you most aware of God's presence (in you, in the other person, between you) in the midst of the conversation?

b. What interrupted or diminished the quality of your presence to God or to the other person?

c. What was the greatest challenge of this experience for you?

FOR THE SPEAKER

a. What was the gift of the conversation for you?

b. What in the listener's manner helped or hindered your ability to pay attention to your life experience and God's presence in it?

c. When were you most aware of God's presence (in you, in the other person, or between you) in the midst of the conversation?

Leader's Notes

CONTRASTS IN HELPING RELATIONSHIPS

Many therapists and counselors are beginning to value the need for transcendence and a sense of the sacred. The contrasts between psychotherapy, counseling, and spiritual guidance are therefore becoming increasingly blurred. Imagine that dotted lines separate the columns below to display graphically this changing awareness. Certainly, each of these helping relationships requires of the helper listening love, authenticity, willingness to enter the world of the other with empathy, and respect for uniqueness.

Psychotherapy	Counseling	Spiritual Guidance
	The process begins in:	
Experience of *confusion* about one's behavior, mental processes, moods, inability to cope and relate in work and love because of unconscious factors.	The need to make choices about life situations and relationships and to remove obstacles to goals adopted. Most issues available to awareness.	Yearning for *coherence* and *communion*. Searching for God and personal meaning. A sense of shallowness or loss of soul and disillusionment.
	The goal tends to be:	
Awareness and reduction of conflict, integration within, increased ability and willingness to function in love and work, increase in "sanity" and ego-control. Good functioning of total physical organism.	Recognition of needs and value, priorities through focus on feelings and increased self-awareness so that decisions can be realistic and lead to satisfaction of self-in-relationships.	Continuous conversion; letting go of resistance to discovery of deeper identity evoked by God. Ego is reduced: "Now I live, no longer I, but Christ lives in me" (Gal. 2:20). Desiring and choosing differently, e.g. the Beatitudes.
	The attitude of the helper is:	
To desire to heal, cure; to comprehend or solve mystery, and to help the person to intrapsychic peace and personal fulfillment. Looking to biochemical causation of the confused state, if biologically oriented.	To work collaboratively with the client so that "will" and ego-management is strengthened, leading to personal achievement of goals chosen. Encourage self-direction and self-assertion in action.	To be in dialogue together in the presence of mystery; willingness for God's intention to be realized through surrender of self-definition. Courageous service leading to universal fulfillment.

Reprinted from an article by Roy Fairchild, published in *Quarterly Review*, vol. 5, no. 2 (summer 1985) and used by permission.

Part 5, Week 2
Spiritual Companions

PREPARATION

Prepare yourself spiritually. Read the material for Week 2 of Part 5, do all the exercises, and keep a journal along with the participants. Pray for each participant and for your leadership, that you may be open to the guidance of the Holy Spirit.

Prepare materials and the room. Read all the material related to the Clearness Committee (pages 167–68), and be prepared to bring an actual discernment issue to the group for the process described in "Deeper Explorations." Contact a group member to be the facilitator or clerk in the Clearness Committee, and share with that person the Leader's Notes so that he or she will be prepared to serve in this role. Select songs or hymns for this session. Make sure you have appropriate hymnals and songbooks. Arrange chairs around a center table and candle.

Review the intent of this meeting: that participants continue to deepen their understanding of spiritual guidance through a small-group experience of the Quaker practice of a Clearness Committee.

OPENING (10 MINUTES)

Welcome all participants personally as they enter.

Set a context.

This is our second meeting of five on the nature and practice of spiritual guidance. This week we move into the arena of group guidance, various forms of which we will continue to explore for the remainder of this final part of *Companions in Christ*.

Join together in worship.

- Light a candle to remind us of the active, illuminating presence of the Holy Spirit in our midst.

- Read John 14:25-27 prayerfully. Repeat verse 26. Affirm that the Spirit's work within and among us is to remind us of the deep truths Jesus taught and embodied. We can trust this work of grace in our midst and be at peace because of it. Invite a few moments of silent reflection for absorbing an atmosphere of trust and peace.

- Offer a brief prayer, entrusting the group time and process to God's gracious purposes.

- Sing a song or hymn that celebrates the reality of God's spirit such as "Sweet, Sweet Spirit"; "Holy Spirit, Truth Divine"; or "Come Down, O Love Divine."

SHARING INSIGHTS (45 MINUTES)

Ask the group members to identify where they have experienced God's presence in their lives this past week. It might help to refer to the examen exercise based on the Lord's Prayer and to allow persons to share their responses.

Invite sharing around the daily exercises.

- Give participants a moment to look over their journals and identify what spoke most deeply to them.

- Encourage them to be listeners: Practice listening to God in each person's reflections and story.

- As leader, model sharing by offering your response first (very briefly) or invite any participant who wishes to do so to begin the sharing.

- Focus on what it means to confirm the "deepest thing" in one another. Encourage participants to reflect on how they see confirmation of the "deepest thing" in the daily scripture readings and how they have experienced this affirmation personally.

- After all have shared, invite the group to identify any patterns or themes that surfaced.

BREAK (10 MINUTES)

Deeper Explorations (45 minutes)

Set a context for exploring the theme of spiritual care and guidance with a small group (5 minutes).

- Help the group see the distinction between spiritual support groups and groups devoted to supporting the Spirit in one another.

- In the first, the primary aim is to support and care for one another directly in our struggles and offer encouragement as Christian friends. In the second type of group, the primary aim is to support the life of the Spirit in us and help us notice and receive God's guidance.

- Any Christian friendship or support group can become deliberate about this important element of spiritual support.

- Discuss examples of each if time permits.

Introduce the Quaker Clearness Committee and review the guidelines (10 minutes).

- **The Quaker Clearness Committee exemplifies a group whose purpose is to support the Spirit in a person and assist that person's desire to discern the direction of the Spirit for his or her life.**

- **The Clearness Committee is based on faith that a Guide is already present and active within us who seeks to lead us in grace and truth. Persons facing an important life question may call a meeting for clearness in order to seek the mind of the Spirit in the company of trusted friends.**

- Review with the group your insights from the Leader's Notes found on pages 167–68. Help participants understand how a Clearness Committee becomes an arena for discernment.

- Present your discernment issue to the group for the focus of the Clearness Committee work. Come prepared to allow the group to help you find clarity.

- Introduce the role of facilitator or clerk to the group. (Remember to have briefed a group member for this role in advance of the meeting.)

Allow the clerk to lead the group as a Clearness Committee (20 minutes minimum).

- The clerk begins the meeting with prayer for each person's openness to the Spirit.

- The clerk asks you to present the issue you are bringing to the group for discernment.

- Following a brief period of silence, the clerk invites group members to ask loving, helpful questions.

- Remember that you have the freedom to answer or to pass on sensitive questions.

- The clerk helps group members honor the guidelines regarding questions and length of speech.

- Conclude the meeting by summarizing what was helpful and whether you gained some degree of clarity from the process. If you did, celebrate and give thanks to God. If not, then ask the group for continued prayer. Another option is to ask the group if they will meet again to continue the process beyond the scheduled bounds of this course.

Take time for the group and you to evaluate the experience (10 minutes).

- **What helped and hindered the process of discernment?**

- **What might have made it more helpful?**

- **What does the experience teach us about spiritual guidance in the community, specifically in small groups?**

Closing (10 minutes)

Sing together several stanzas of the song you sang in the "Opening" or another selection.

Pray. Invite spoken prayers of thanksgiving or supplication, as participants feel moved.

Offer a benediction.

(Be sure to thank your clerk!)

Leader's Notes

CLEARNESS COMMITTEE

The Clearness Committee is a structure for dealing with our dilemmas in the company of a few friends who can help us seek God's direction. Historically, Quakers used the Clearness Committee when two members of a local meeting (congregation) asked to be married. In the twentieth century, Quakers expanded the approach to help individuals make a variety of important decisions.

Behind the Clearness Committee is a simple but crucial spiritual conviction: Each of us has an inner, divine light that gives us the guidance we need but is often obscured by sundry forms of inner and outer interference. The function of the Clearness Committee is not to give advice or alter or "fix" people but to help people remove obstacles and discover the divine assistance that is within. Rooted in that conviction, the Clearness Committee can help people discover their own God-given leadings and callings through silence, questioning, listening, and prayer.

1. The person seeking clearness writes down his or her situation in advance of the meeting and circulates the statement to committee members. The issue should be identified as precisely as possible. This is the focus person's first step toward "clearness."

2. The focus person chooses his or her committee—five or six trusted individuals with as much diversity among them as possible. The committee should meet with the understanding that there may be a second and even a third meeting in subsequent weeks.

3. A "clerk" (facilitator) is named to open the meeting, close it, and serve as a "traffic cop," making sure that the rules are followed and that everyone who wants to speak can get in.

4. Typically, the meeting begins with a period of centering silence. The focus person begins with a fresh summary of the issue. Then committee members speak, governed by a simple but demanding rule: Members must limit themselves to asking the focus person questions—honest, caring questions. This means no advice ("Why don't you . . . ?" or "My uncle had the same problem and he . . ." or "I know a good

therapist that could help."), only authentic, challenging, open, loving questions. Members guard against questions that arise from curiosity rather than care for the person's clarity about his or her inner truth. The clerk dismisses questions that are advice or judgment in disguise.

5. Committee members should try to ask questions briefly and to the point. The focus person usually responds to questions as they are asked, keeping responses relatively brief. It is always the focus person's right, however, not to answer in order to protect privacy.

6. The pacing of the questioning and answering should be relaxed, gentle, and humane. Do not be afraid of silence in the group.

7. The Clearness Committee works best when everyone approaches it in a prayerful mood, inwardly affirming the reality of each person's inner guidance and truth. We must give up the pretense that we can know another's truth or that we are obliged to "save" each other. Rather, we help one another pay attention to God's saving and guiding presence.

The Clearness Committee is a powerful way to rally the strength of community around a struggling soul, drawing deeply on "that of God" within each of us. The Clearness Committee has its dangers. But once the spiritual discipline is understood and embraced, it becomes a new channel for the spirit of God to move with grace and power in our midst.

Adapted from the article "The Clearness Committee: A Way of Discernment" by Parker J. Palmer, included in the book *Communion, Community, Commonweal* (Nashville, Tenn.: Upper Room Books, 1995), 131–36.

Part 5, Week 3
Small Groups for Spiritual Guidance

PREPARATION

Prepare yourself spiritually. Read the material for Week 3 of Part 5, do all the exercises, and keep a journal along with the participants. Pray that God will prepare you and each participant to receive the greatest benefit from your group meeting.

Prepare materials and the room. Select songs and gather hymnals/songbooks. Arrange the room. Select a group member to assist in the group exercise on accountable discipleship. Give that person an overview of how such groups function so that he or she will be prepared to lead such a group. This member's familiarity with the covenant discipleship group model will be helpful. Set the chairs in a circle with a center table and candle. Prepare on newsprint a rough sketch of the church as a garden, built on the image from Catherine of Siena found on page 259 in the Participant's Book (Part 5, p. 41). Don't worry about making an artistic image; try to catch the basic symbol in some way. The group will add to it during the closing worship. You will need some colored pencils or markers for the closing worship as well as some tacks or tape to hang the drawing in a centrally visible place.

Review the intent of the meeting: that participants experience the support and guidance of a small group focused on the ways we hold one another accountable in our discipleship.

OPENING (10 MINUTES)

Welcome all participants personally as they enter.

Set the context.

This is our third meeting on spiritual guidance and our second focused on group expressions of such guidance. In the second half of our time together, we will experience a taste of the highly mutual covenant discipleship model of small-group guidance.

Join together in worship.

- Light a candle to remind us of the ever-present light of Christ in the midst of our gathering.

- Prayerfully read Matthew 18:19-20.

- Invite people to a few minutes of silent prayer. Ask them to be aware of one another together in the light of Christ and to sense the power of common purpose that is given to gathered believers in and through the Holy Spirit.

- Now invite prayers to be spoken aloud from the silence.

- Conclude with a song or hymn of your choosing.

SHARING INSIGHTS (45 MINUTES)

Ask the group members to identify where they have experienced God's presence in their lives this past week. Allow time for persons to respond to the examen exercise (# 5), as they feel led.

Invite sharing around the daily exercises.

- Give participants a moment to look over their journals and identify what seemed to be most challenging to them in the daily exercises. Focus on each person's insights and experiences of the power of living in community as seen in the pattern of Christ. Invite participants to think about how we grow in our ability to be shaped by the Spirit in community. How do we experience the power of community in Christ?

- Encourage them to be listeners: Practice listening for God in each person's reflections and story.

- As leader, model sharing by offering your response first (very briefly) or invite any participant who wishes to do so to begin the sharing.

- After all have shared, invite the group to identify any patterns or themes that surfaced.

BREAK (10 MINUTES)

DEEPER EXPLORATIONS (45 MINUTES)

Set a context for an accountable discipleship meeting (7 minutes).

- The word *covenant* means to be shackled together as persons who row a boat together. We journey forward in Christ in the company of one another. A beautiful image is that of the redwood trees whose roots are not so remarkably deep for their tremendous height but are intertwined in a way that makes them strong for one another; their interconnected roots give them the support they need to stand. We watch over one another in love "that we may walk in the way that leads to life."

- Invite everyone to read the General Rule of Discipleship found on pages 298–99 of the Participant's Book (Part 5, pp. 73–74). Explore the group's responses to this image of the Christian life.

- Explain that the early Methodist societies helped people find the path that leads to life by defining a General Rule emphasizing "works of mercy" (doing all the good you can, avoiding all harm) and "works of piety" (praying, searching scripture, fasting, Christian conferencing or conversation, being temperate, and receiving Holy Communion).

- Today covenant discipleship groups translate the original "General Rule of the United Societies" into a contemporary General Rule of Discipleship that calls for discipline in four areas: worship and devotion, justice and compassion.

- Covenant discipleship groups begin by working together to form agreements that express the rule of Christian discipleship in ways that have meaning for them. The group meets weekly for one hour to account for how they are living their covenant and to watch over one another in love. Ask everyone to look at a sample covenant that was written by one group in the Participant's Book, page 300 (Part 5, p. 75).

Lead an accountable discipleship meeting (30 minutes).

- Form two smaller groups of four or five in order to make the most of the time. You will serve as leader of one small group, and the second group will be led by the group member you have selected and briefed in advance (see notes under "Preparation").

- Ask all participants to keep in front of them the General Rule of Discipleship and the sample covenant. Explain that, for purposes of this meeting, we will let the image of the General Rule serve as a basis for the group to experience the accountable discipleship group model.

- Beginning with "acts of compassion," invite group members to take turns saying what that quadrant means for them and reporting on how they are doing with it. After all have shared around the "compassion" quadrant, focus on the "acts of justice" quadrant, and so on.

- Help group members watch the time and move along in their reporting, but be careful not to rush anyone or to force a completion of all four quadrants in thirty minutes.

- Draw the meeting to a close by asking persons to indicate where they plan to deepen their discipleship in the week to come and areas where they need the prayers and support of the group.

Gather the two groups together to evaluate the meeting (8 minutes).

Ask group members to name:

- What did you find most helpful and promising?

- What did you find least helpful?

- What other component would you want as part of an ongoing covenant group experience?

Closing (10 minutes)

Remind the group of the image of the garden used by Catherine of Siena from the Participant's Book. Catherine records that God speaks of the church as a great vineyard in which each individual has his or her own vine garden but no fences or dividing lines exist between the gardens. Whatever happens in one's own vineyard, for good or for ill, intimately affects every other vineyard.

Hold up your unfinished sketch of this image and tape or tack it to a flip chart or wall. Spread out colored pencils or markers. Invite people to take a few colors, come forward, and add to the picture some symbol of how they see the covenant community as a "garden" of spiritual guidance.

Recall the image of the redwood trees whose roots are intertwined and hold one another in place. It is another helpful image for what it means to live as companions in Christ and in covenant with God, watching over one another in love. Is there anything else people would like to add to the picture?

Close by praying together the Covenant Prayer found on page 301 of the Participant's Book (Part 5, p. 76). You might also wish to sing the "Companion Song."

Part 5, Week 4

Re-Visioning Our Life As Companions in Christ

PREPARATION

Prepare yourself spiritually. Read the material for Week 4 of Part 5, do all the exercises, and keep a journal along with the participants. Spend time in prayer seeking God's guidance for the group meeting, and pray for each participant.

Prepare materials and the room. Choose songs and gather appropriate hymnals and song-books. Set chairs in a circle with a center table and candle.

Review the intent of the meeting: that group members continue to explore God's ways of guiding us in our personal and community life and that group members might experience a model of small-group discernment.

OPENING (10 MINUTES)

Welcome all group members personally as they enter.

Set the context.

This is the fourth of five meetings on spiritual guidance and the next to last of our covenanted meetings in *Companions in Christ*. We continue to explore other aspects of group spiritual guidance, including a process of discernment in the second half of our time together.

Join together in worship.

- Light a candle to remind us of the discerning light and wisdom of God's spirit in our midst.

- Prayerfully read John 16:12-13. Invite the group to ponder these words and contemplate what new truths the Spirit has led Christians to understand since Christ walked this earth.

Remind people that any process of discerning God's truth in our time is based on the promise contained in this text.

- Allow a time for prayers of thanksgiving and supplication as people feel moved.

- Sing a few stanzas of a song or hymn asking for guidance such as "Have Thine Own Way"; "Savior, Like a Shepherd Lead Us"; "Seek Ye First"; "Dear Lord, Lead Me Day by Day"; or "Day by Day."

SHARING INSIGHTS (45 MINUTES)

Ask the group members to identify where they have experienced God's presence in their lives this past week.

Invite sharing around the daily exercises.

- Give participants a moment to review their journals.

- Ask group members to select an exercise and to share from their journals. Be sure to give all members an opportunity to share insights on decision making in their personal lives and in the church.

- Encourage them to be listeners: Practice listening for God in each person's reflections and story.

- As leader, model sharing by offering your response first (very briefly) or invite any participant who wishes to do so to begin the sharing.

- After all have shared, invite the group to identify any patterns or themes that surfaced.

BREAK (10 MINUTES)

DEEPER EXPLORATIONS (45 MINUTES)

Set a context (10 minutes).

- **In this course, we have focused largely on prayerful discernment of God's presence and call in our personal lives. This week, we are focusing on corporate discernment, or what it means to seek God's will together as a community.**

- Invite the group to name some of the ways we typically seek direction and make decisions in the church. Examples might include the following: using reasoned discourse, following the leader, pleasing as many as possible, experiencing extraordinary revelations, doing what the Bible says, building consensus, allowing the majority to rule, following parliamentary procedure, doing business as usual, and so on. Which approaches to decision making are typical in your church?

- **The practice that belongs uniquely to the church is prayerful discernment. It is based on biblical faith that God loves us and longs to lead us on the path that leads to life. In prayerful discernment, we trust that Christ is head of his body, the church. We depend on the Spirit to know us and guide us in all matters affecting Christ's life and ministry in, among, and through us. When we practice prayerful discernment, God can build up the community in love even as we work through differences in search of God's will. An approach to prayerful discernment is an antidote to the adversarial path prescribed by parliamentary procedure and majority rule.**

Introduce an exercise in seeking God's will together (5 minutes).

Here are two options:

1. Introduce a real issue in your congregation that concerns everyone. Write up the issue in simple language for the group to consider.

2. Or imagine a scenario in which the group is a church leadership council. In this scenario, a team from among the group was sent out to prayerfully consider the future direction of our common ministry. The team returned with a simple proposal for the council to consider (two alternative versions are printed in the box on the next page). Now the council will approach the proposal as a matter for discernment.

PROPOSAL

We propose that every aspect of congregational life be approached in light of the mission of our church: "to make disciples of Jesus Christ for the transformation of the world." Activities that do not support or further this mission will be eliminated or transformed.

or

We propose that every aspect of congregational life be designed and approached with the intention of helping people grow toward maturity in the Christian life, through increasing participation in the heart, mind, and work of Christ. Activities and settings that do not support and further this mission will be eliminated or transformed.

Lead the group through the first few steps of the prayerful discernment process (30 minutes). (Refer to the Leader's Notes on "Steps for Prayerful Discernment," pages 177–78.) Remind the participants that the Steps or Principles are found on page 278 of the Participant's Book (Part 5, p. 60). End your time together by allowing group members to reflect on this experience.

CLOSING (10 MINUTES)

Sing together a few stanzas of a song or hymn of your choosing, perhaps focused on thanksgiving.

What have we learned? Allow each person to share some insight or discovery from this meeting.

Pray together: Invite spoken prayers as participants feel moved.

Sing or say a benediction.

Leader's Notes

STEPS FOR PRAYERFUL DISCERNMENT

The following are suggestions for guiding your group through the prayerful discernment exercise. Though you will not have time to complete more than a few steps, try to move at least through the step called "shedding." Enter the process seriously as a realistic effort in discernment. As leader, select prior to the meeting from one of the two options outlined on pages 175–76. You will present your selection during the framing part of the exercise.

Framing: If you selected an issue from your church life, help the group focus on a current question or dilemma in your church that concerns almost everyone in the group and will be quickly understood by everyone. If you selected the second option, choose one of the suggested proposals and help the group get in touch with the potential impact of the proposed policy. Discuss some of the implications of its application on things that affect them, such as a church basketball team, the way the finance committee meets, etc.

Grounding: Invite the group members to think about a guiding principle that would set appropriate boundaries for their deliberations the way the shoulder of a highway keeps cars heading the right direction. The idea is that any adequate answer should line up with the guiding principle. For example, a parent may ask, "What food should I prepare for my children?" and answer it with a variety of possibilities so long as they align with a guiding principle such as, "A balance of foods with adequate nutrition." A guiding principle on a church matter could be a brief mission statement or a statement of intent such as: "that all we do will help people grow toward maturity in the Christian life."

Shedding: Ask the group members to name any feelings, fears, or prejudgments that could limit their willingness to entertain positions other than their own. Challenge each person to wrestle with the test of "indifference": As I enter into this process, am I prepared to say that I am indifferent to everything but God's will? Shedding is critical for proceeding honestly and fruitfully with any discernment process, so take as long as necessary. Shedding may require silent reflection, prayer, honest confession, and heartfelt sharing to prepare the way for the Lord.

Rooting: Invite the group members to recall texts from the Bible (scripture), wisdom from our spiritual heritage (tradition), and experiences from our walk with God (experience) that relate in their minds to the issue (reason). Explore the connections they see or feel. Trust the leading of the Spirit and seek the light of truth.

Listening: Consider additional voices the group needs to hear.

Exploring: Consider all of the options and paths within the guiding principle.

Improving: Labor together to make each option the best it can be, even those options that you do not like. Seek to improve options with the intent of offering your best to God.

Weighing: Offer your best options to God, one at a time, weighing your readiness as a group to acknowledge a preference for a particular proposal.

Closing: Going around the room, ask each to declare his or her level of acceptance of a proposed path. Invite everyone also to register any lingering concerns.

Resting: Hold the decision in silence; keep it near your hearts in prayer. Does the group as a whole have a sense of assurance or anxiousness, consolation or desolation? Do you feel that the decision seems "good to the Holy Spirit and to us" (Acts 15:25)?

Adapted from *Discerning God's Will Together* by Danny E. Morris and Charles M. Olsen (Nashville, Tenn.: The Upper Room, 1997), 66–67.

Part 5, Week 5
Discerning Our Need for Guidance

PREPARATION

Prepare yourself spiritually. Read the material for Week 5 of Part 5, do all the exercises, and keep a journal along with the participants. Spend time in prayer for openness to God's presence and guidance of the Spirit in your meeting time.

Prepare materials and the room. Select songs and needed hymnals or songbooks. Arrange the room with a center table and candle. Bring newsprint or poster board for preparing a large sketch of the concentric circles, Participant's Book, page 302 (Part 5, p. 77). Bring sticky notes in two colors for the participants' use during the "Deeper Explorations." Be prepared to announce the arrangements (time and place, etc.) for the closing retreat if you have not yet done so.

Review the intent of this meeting: that participants explore current reality in their congregation and begin to re-vision new possibilities and settings for God's guidance and nurture.

OPENING (10 MINUTES)

Welcome all group members personally as they enter.

Set a context.

This is our final meeting focused on spiritual guidance and the last regular meeting of *Companions in Christ.* It will be a special gathering and an important one in which we look at the mission and ministries of our congregation in light of what we have been learning together here.

Join together in worship.

- Begin by lighting the Christ candle, a sign of God's faithful presence in our midst from the beginning of our time together.

- Invite silent reflection on the gifts of these many weeks as companions in Christ.

- Invite prayers of gratitude and petition as people are moved.

- Sing a hymn or song of thanksgiving and praise. Let the group suggest a favorite!

SHARING INSIGHTS (45 MINUTES)

Ask the group members to identify where they have experienced God's presence in their lives this past week.

Invite sharing around the daily exercises.

- After giving time for all the group members to look over their journals, ask them to share first in response to Exercise 3.

- As leader, model sharing by offering your response first (very briefly) or invite any participant who wishes to do so to begin the sharing.

- Continue to encourage them to be listeners.

- After all have shared, invite the group to identify any patterns or themes that surfaced.

BREAK (10 MINUTES)

DEEPER EXPLORATIONS (45 MINUTES)

Set the context for exploring the church as an ecology of spiritual care and guidance (10 minutes).

- Refer to the quote from Susanne Johnson at the beginning of the daily exercises for this week. Ask the group, **What does the word** *ecology* **suggest to you? What images come to mind?** Consider the various responses of the group.

- Then encourage the group to explore the ecology (organic, interrelated, or multileveled nature) of spiritual care and guidance in our congregation.

- Ask the group to look at the illustration of concentric circles of guidance in the church that is found in the Participant's Book page 302 (Part 5, p. 77). Refer to the quotations from Susanne Johnson found on pages 302–303 (Part 5, pp. 77–78). Invite the group members to lift out words and phrases that they like or wonder about.

Lead an exercise in exploring the promise of spiritual guidance in your church (35 minutes).

• Introduce the exercise: **This is an exercise in beginning to seek God's call and direction for our congregation as an environment of spiritual care and guidance. The exercise involves some assessing of current reality, some envisioning of possibilities, and listening for the voice of God's truth and guidance for us.**

• Post a rough sketch of the concentric circles on the wall or board using newsprint or poster board.

• Lead the group through the exercise in the following manner and in your own words:

   1. *Name current reality.* **In solitude, ponder the sketch on the wall of the concentric circles of guidance in the church. Write on sticky notes (one thought per note) the name of each active setting for spiritual care and guidance in the congregation that you know about. Identify in your mind the one that has been or is most important for you and why.** (Be sure that everyone uses the same color sticky notes for this part of the exercise. Allow two to three minutes for persons to write their notes.)

      As a group, take turns sharing where you see active settings of spiritual guidance in your church. As you share the settings that you have identified, place your sticky notes into the concentric circle to which they best relate. Identify the one setting that has been most meaningful for you and why.

   2. *See the promise.* **Now write on a different color sticky note other possible settings for spiritual care and guidance in your church that you believe people need in order to continue to mature in the Christian life. Identify in your mind the one you feel most strongly about and why.** (Be sure that each person uses the same color for this part of the exercise. Allow three to five minutes.)

      Now share your responses with the group in the same manner as before. Name each possibility as you post it in a particular circle. Also identify the one possibility about which you feel most strongly and why.

   3. *Reflect on the picture and the gift God has given us here.* **Look at the many settings for guidance represented. How would you characterize the different kinds of guidance represented here? What does our chart say about what kinds of guidance are most and least available, most and least needed at this time?**

What Bible stories or hymns come to mind that celebrate the reality and promise we have depicted on the chart?

4. *Listen for the voice of the Spirit, our Counselor and Guide.* Let's be silent for two minutes. Listen again in your mind to the concerns, hopes, and testimonies that you have heard during this time together and listen for how God may be speaking to us through these words. What word, insight, or image continues to reverberate within you regarding the promise of our church as a community of grace and guidance? (Allow two to three minutes of silence.)

CLOSING (10 MINUTES)

Relight the candle.

Invite sharing: What word, question, promise, or challenge has the Spirit spoken to your heart as we looked at possibilities for our church? Let's listen to one another prayerfully and without commentary. Listen for the promise for spiritual guidance in our church.

Invite prayer. Offer prayers based on what has just been shared, as you feel moved.

Sing together a few stanzas of one of the hymns brought to mind earlier during the "Deeper Explorations." (If no hymns or songs were mentioned, have a few options in mind.)

Remember: This is just the beginning of re-visioning our church. Let's continue to ponder the promise, listen for God's call, and ask ourselves what all this means about the way we participate and lead in the congregation. We will return to this issue in our final retreat.

Sing a doxology!

Closing Retreat for 28-Week *Companions in Christ*

PREPARATION

Prepare materials. Select songs/hymns for use in worship, and choose scripture readings or use the suggested text. Review the whole retreat: decide how to introduce the storytelling segment, and familiarize yourself with the guided meditation. Preprint questions for the 11:30 AM segment on Saturday. Select a Communion liturgy familiar to your group. (Make copies of the liturgy or use one printed in a hymnbook.) Develop what you want to say and how you want to lead people into reflection through the closing homily. Review your own journal in preparation. If you are not ordained, invite a pastor/priest to celebrate Communion with the group. Have blank paper for writing testimonies. After the retreat, please copy and complete the evaluation sheet found on page 239 and return it to the following address: *Companions in Christ*, Upper Room Ministries, P.O. Box 340004, Nashville, TN 37203-0012.

Note: You can easily adapt the time frames of this retreat to fit your local needs and traditions. Timing will also vary depending on the group size. With more adaptation and trimming, it may fit into a single longer day. There is real benefit, however, in allowing the group's integration and discernment process to "percolate" overnight. Unless your group desires an experience away from home, this retreat can easily take place at the group's regular meeting site with participants going home for the night.

Prepare meeting space. Select the retreat site (church, the group's regular meeting place, or outside center). Arrange in advance the handling in a timely way of supper, breakfast foods, and lunch (church volunteers outside of group, catered/boxed meals, or meals provided by retreat or other facility). Prepare the group meeting space so it is comfortable. Arrange a worship center/table with beauty and simplicity in mind (cloth, candles, cross, perhaps fresh flowers, or an icon).

Prepare yourself spiritually. Pray for God's grace to bless and guide the retreat day. Ask the Spirit to prepare each participant, including yourself, to receive God's best purposes for your closing time together.

Developing a Rule of Life

Suggested Time Frame: Friday Evening 6:00–9:30, Saturday 8AM–3:30PM

FRIDAY EVENING

PART 1: CELEBRATION!

6:00   **Gather for supper** (Arrange ahead for potluck or other easy fare)

7:00   **Worship**

Invite silence for centering; meditative music optional

Light the Christ candle and say these words:

> We are gathered in the living presence of Christ once again. Our retreat marks the end of this *Companions* experience but not the end of our being companions in Christ. We now have a chance to reflect on where we have come by God's grace in these weeks together and where we perceive the call to continued spiritual practice in our own lives and in our church. Through this retreat each of us will begin to frame a personal rule of life to support our ongoing spiritual journeys. We will look for ways to encourage one another in the commitments we make.

Sing or play a hymn or song. Choose a song that your group particularly likes to sing.

Read a psalm, followed by silence. Suggestions: Psalm 36:5-9; Psalm 84; Psalm 89:1-5; Psalm 100; or Psalm 150.

Offer a prayer of gratitude for what Companions *has meant,* and ask that God's purpose be fulfilled in each person present and the congregation(s) represented.

7:15   **"Telling our Story"** (1 hour and 45 minutes maximum)

Introduce a process of review, reflection and sharing:

We are going to review each part of our Companions book and journal to identify what has been most meaningful and effective for us. As we do this, we'll be telling the story of our time together, celebrating the wonderful gifts we have received, and preparing to discern where God is drawing us forward.

Review each part:

Let's look back at Part 1, "Embracing the Journey," to see what really stood out for us at the beginning of this group experience. As you look back, especially at your journal, what were the best daily exercises for you? What was most meaningful in our small group meeting times? *(Allow 5 minutes for review)*

Invite responses (10 minutes)

Additional questions to ask:

How many of you came to enjoy journaling? Even if you didn't really enjoy it, how did you find yourself benefiting from it? Do you plan to continue journaling as a spiritual practice?

Let's go on to Part 2, "Feeding on the Word." Review your journals for that section and notice what especially stood out for you. Which way of reading and praying with scripture really spoke to you or changed your way of relating to the Bible? (Allow 5 minutes for review)

Invite responses (10 minutes)

Additional questions to ask: Which of these approaches to scripture are you most likely to continue to use? Do you use one approach regularly now?

8:00   Break

8:15   *Continue storytelling review:*

Let's turn now to Part 3, "Deepening Our Prayer." Take a few minutes to review your journal pages for what most affected your way of understanding or of practicing prayer. Which particular form of prayer has stayed with you? (5 minutes)

Responses (10 minutes)

Additional questions to ask:

How many of you still use a breath prayer? Which way of prayer do you want to continue using or to explore further?

Let's move on to Part 4, "Responding to our Call." Review your journal exercises and weekly meeting notes. What spoke to you most deeply here? What insights did you gain about your particular gifts or vocation from God? (5 minutes)

Invite responses (10 minutes)

Additional questions to ask:

What particular practices do you associate with this exploration of gifts and call? Which of these would you choose to continue in daily life?

Finally, let's look at Part 5, "Exploring Spiritual Guidance." What was most striking or helpful in these last weeks? What new learning did you glean and which practices would you like to explore further? *(5 minutes)*

Invite responses (10 minutes)

Additional questions to ask:

Which particular form of examen did you find especially helpful? Which one would you most likely use on a daily basis? How can you see holy listening as a regular part of your Christian life? Where do you envision discernment as a helpful tool personally or in the church's life?

Prepare for closing worship: We have been reviewing our experience of the weeks we've had together, telling the story by sharing highlights, insights, and the sense of leading God has stirred among us. What a wonderful story to celebrate! Tomorrow we will continue to integrate what we have learned by discerning practices for a personal rule of life to sustain our spiritual growth. But for now, let's gather up the gifts of this evening in worship.

9:15   Evening Prayers (Select song, scripture: Luke 2:29-32, prayer, blessing; or use a night prayer service from your tradition)

SATURDAY

PART 2: INTEGRATION

8:00   **Gather for tea, coffee, and conversation.**

8:15   **Morning prayers** (Silence, scripture: Psalm 63:1-8, prayer, song, blessing)

8:30   *Lead a reflective process with scripture.*

Read John 21:1-17 in three sections. As you read the scripture, imagine what is taking place; don't rush the story. Invite reflection and journaling as follows:

- *Read verses 1-8:* Indicate that the image of casting the nets on the "right side" of the boat, sometimes translated the "other side," might be seen as an instruction to try something different. *Ask,* **What has been most surprising or unexpected in your experience with** *Companions in Christ.* **Where has God invited you to cast your net on the "other side"? . . . What has come of this? What "catch" have you received in the form of new perspectives or practices? . . .**

  Allow 10 minutes for participants to ponder these questions in silence. Ask them to use their journals to note responses or draw images of their "catch."

- *Read verses 9-14:* Make the point that Jesus not only provides us the catch, he feeds us before asking us to feed others. *Ask,* **How would you describe the way Jesus has fed you over the course of our time together? What has been the flavor and savor of "breakfast on the beach" as a companion in Christ? . . . How do you need to continue to be fed? . . .**

  Allow 10 minutes for participants to respond to these questions in their journals, again with freedom to draw images or symbols.

- *Read verses 15-17.* Point out that Jesus asks us to feed others as a direct expression of our love for him. Invite participants into a brief guided meditation: *(5 minutes)*

  Sit awhile with the risen Christ, aware of having been well fed and loved. . . . Talk with Jesus about his love for you and your love for him; listen to see if he directs you in a particular way. . . . What do you feel called to do as a result of your personal journey through these months with your small group companions? . . . How

can you feed others, given your own particular gifts, sense of vocation, and new-found spiritual practices? . . .

Allow 10 minutes of silence for prayer, reflection, and journaling with these questions.

• *Distribute crayons and paper.* Invite participants to use the hand they usually do not use to draw a quick symbolic impression of what they have received through *Companions in Christ.* (Using the nondominant hand helps release us from anxiety about drawing things "right" or "well." Drawing with our nondominant hand can open us to the symbolic and expressive language of the heart, giving us access to our deeper God-given wisdom.) Then suggest that they draw a second impression of what they feel they have to offer out of this experience. Remind them that this is not about "art" but about getting visual clues about the movement of the Spirit within them. Ask them to keep these images for closing worship. *(5 minutes)*

9:20   **Break**

9:30   **Invite shared responses to the reflection process** *(45 minutes)*

Record on newsprint what has been most striking to group members in terms of the "catch" from *Companions* (insight, practice, mutual support, etc.). Then distill what seems to lie at the heart of participants' needs for further spiritual food and how they feel called to offer their gifts and learning to others. *(25 minutes)*

Bring this section to closure by reading John 21:18-19.

Ask participants to reflect on their level of inner freedom to follow Jesus Christ into an unknown future. Are you willing to let the Spirit lead in whatever comes next? What would it look like to follow Jesus in faith and trust as you move into the days ahead? Invite prayerful reflection on the verses and journaling with the questions. You might play soft instrumental music for this. *(10 minutes)*

Offer a time for sharing (10 minutes)

10:15   **Break**

PART 3: ANTICIPATION

10:30   **Discerning a Rule of Life**   *(50 minutes)*

Set the context. Read Isaiah 43:18-19. Indicate that, like Peter and the disciples at the end of John's Gospel, we are being called to look toward the new future God is creating even now. Do we have eyes to see what our Lord is doing with our lives, personally and for the sake of the church?

Explain briefly the concept of a Rule of Life

Offer the following quote:

> A rule of life is a pattern of spiritual disciplines that provide structure for our growth in holiness.... [It] is not meant to be restrictive, although it certainly asks for genuine commitment. It is meant to help us establish a rhythm of daily living, a basic order within which new freedoms can grow. A rule of life, like a trellis, curbs our tendency to wander and supports our frail efforts to grow spiritually. (M. J. Thompson, *Soul Feast*, 146)

Guide a process of discerning and formulating a rule of life.

We have been assessing which practices over the course of our time together have been most meaningful and transforming, both personally and as a group. Now we have an opportunity to make intentional choices about which of these we feel most drawn to continue in a regular way, and to frame a simple rule of life for ourselves. We might try to think about at least one practice that feels natural to us and one that feels more challenging, stretching us to grow in new ways.

Encourage participants to look over journal responses to the Celebration storytelling review. Ask if they would like to commit on a daily basis to two or three basic spiritual practices, such as *lectio*, prayer, or examen. Invite them to recall practices they have carried forward from one part of *Companions* to the next, as clues to which ones they might want to continue. *(10 minutes)*

Ask participants to consider the best time of day for each practice they wish to build into their lives. Encourage them to offer at least one practice to God in the morning before the day gets too busy, on the principle of greeting Christ first. Invite creative thinking: shower and commute time may be among the more practical possibilities. Ask them to consider one evening practice if possible; examen is especially well-suited for the day's end. *(5 minutes)*

Invite them to ponder a few practices they might incorporate into their rule on a periodic basis, such as discernment, spiritual guidance, small-group formation, or retreat. How often (weekly, monthly, annually) would they choose these practices? *(10 minutes)*

Have them formulate a pattern of commitments they feel they can realistically make at this point in their lives. This becomes the first draft of a personal rule of life. Encourage them not to get carried away with too many commitments but to "start small." *(5 minutes)*

Share in pairs.   *(15 minutes)*

Invite everyone to pair with another group member who will be offering support through prayer and encouragement. Join with another yourself or with a pair to form a triad; as leader, it is important for you to participate in this process.

Share rule of life drafts. The listening partner should feel free to ask clarifying questions. Pairs will discuss and choose a few simple ways to support each other in the practice of their rule (examples: share copies of their rules, weekly phone calls, encouraging notes, daily prayer, monthly lunches).

Have partners offer prayer for each other to close this time together.

11:20   **Break** *(keep it brief)*

11:30   **Discerning the body of Christ** *(45 minutes)*

> Now it's time to think together about expanding from our personal commitment to helping our church grow spiritually. How might our learning from *Companions* encourage our congregation and its leaders to deepen their journeys?

Invite a few minutes of quiet reflection on each of the following questions. Preprint questions on two pieces of newsprint, leaving space to record responses below each question. *(15 minutes)*

> What practices have we tried that could gradually transform the way our church functions in its commitments, activities, and decisions?

> How can we share our growth and sense of call in an inviting way?

Ask if anyone feels called and ready to begin a new spiritual ministry in the church. Preprint the ideas listed below, with additional newsprint for ideas from the group. *(20 minutes)*

- Become a leader or coleader for a new *Companions in Christ* group

- Start a weekly group for *lectio divina*, perhaps on the preacher's main text
- Gather and guide an intercessory prayer group, or organize a prayer chain based on prayer requests collected during Sunday worship
- Teach a class on discerning spiritual gifts and vocation for new members
- Start a group or class of church members interested in sharing their ongoing spiritual journeys and supporting one another through prayerful encouragement
- Volunteer to teach the discernment process to a church committee chair

Elicit ideas from the group.

Allow connections to surface between group members who may feel called to similar ministries and give them a little time to confer together. Pay attention to where energy surfaces in the group or among particular members, and encourage that energy to find creative expression. If one or two people are ready to start something, gather the group around them to offer a short prayer and blessing.

Ask if all or some participants want to continue meeting as a group for a period of time. (10 minutes)

Find a meeting time to choose resources and a group process. You might meet over lunch, or determine a time after the retreat. Name several group models to consider: another resource in the Companions series, beginning a *Weavings* Reading Group, selecting a book or workbook to study, continuing as a *lectio* or intercessory prayer group, gathering monthly for a healing service or local mission project. If meeting in the near future, identify a volunteer to gather and distribute information on the options so participants can consider possibilities before the designated meeting. Indicate that the location and frequency of meetings (weekly, twice a month, or monthly) will be decided at that meeting.

12:15   Lunch and rest or walk

PART 4: NEXT GENERATION

1:30   Sharing our witness *(45 minutes)*

Set the context. Read Isaiah 55:10-11.

It is time to listen for how God's word spoken among us may accomplish the larger divine purpose. We cannot know all that our gracious Lord intends, but as friends of Christ we can offer ourselves to his continued labor of healing and redemption.

How, then, shall we share the bread we have been given through *Companions*? Who in our circle of acquaintances might be ready for the *Companions* experience, even if they don't yet know it?

First, we will write our "witness to the next generation"—letters, stories, or notes of encouragement for those who will next choose to go through *Companions in Christ*.

Pass out paper; testimonies will be brought forward as an offering in the closing worship, and collected for publicizing and recruiting new *Companions* groups.

Allow participants to write testimonies (15 minutes)

Share testimonies aloud as people feel led (20 minutes)

Pray for future companions in Christ and for their leaders (5 minutes)

2:15   Break

2:30   Closing Worship (May incorporate abbreviated Communion or an Agape meal)

Suggestion: Develop a short homily (8–10 minutes) based on the theme of "adverse winds" or "headwinds" in Mark 6:45-52. Use the following guidelines:

The context of this passage is the miraculous feeding of the five thousand (draw parallels between the passage and this time of transition and closure for us, and how we have been fed).

When the disciples find themselves in the midst of a storm, they quickly forget the miracle they have just experienced and allow anxiety to grip them. Even when Jesus comes to them through the adverse winds, they think he is a ghost (unreal). This could easily happen to us if we lose our focus on the presence and reality of Christ in daily life.

Invite reflection: What "adverse winds" might we anticipate that could make us lose heart, forget our experience here, distract our focus from Christ—even to the point that we might imagine what we have experienced here was a "ghost," not quite real? What steps can we take to anticipate and counter the headwinds of life?

Share in pairs around these two questions, and pray for each other.

Remember to invite participants to bring forward their testimonies and their two drawings from the John 21 reflection as offerings. Testimonies might be collected in a basket, while the drawings might be spread on a table for visual impact.

Suggestion: Use Isaiah 55:12-13 as a benediction.

Note: This worship could be completed in about thirty minutes without a Communion or Agape service and could last up to an hour with one or the other. Set the time for good-byes accordingly, between 3:00 and 3:30PM.

Solitary Reflection Questions
FOLLOWING THE GUIDED MEDITATION ON JOHN 21:1-19

How have I/we been fed through *Companions in Christ*? What have we "caught"?

What do we sense that we are drawn by the Spirit to continue? How might we do it (either personally and/or together)?

How might we offer something of what we have received to our congregation?

Getting Started Guide

This Getting Started Guide will help you promote, recruit, encourage, and sustain *Companions in Christ*. It includes suggestions to help you start a spiritual formation group that we believe can change lives and strengthen your congregation. The suggestions that follow are for use with starting 28-week *Companions* groups.

Promotion

What Is
Companions in Christ?

Companions in Christ is

- a small group of people praying together.

- an opportunity for daily individual reading and reflection.

- a focus on how you experience God.

- a group supporting your spiritual growth.

- a group reaching out to other *Companions* groups.

- an opportunity to learn various styles and forms of prayer.

- a record or journal of your walk with Christ.

- an invitation to let scripture form your faith.

- a time to reflect on where God is calling you and to affirm the gifts God has given you.

- a discovery of spiritual friends who will listen to and pray for you.

What Is a Spiritual Formation Group?

Through *Companions in Christ,*

- You will explore the depths of scripture, learn to listen to God through it, and allow your life to be shaped by the Word.

- You will experience new dimensions of prayer, try fresh ways of opening to God, and learn what it means to practice the presence of God.

- You will reflect on Christ's call in your life and discover anew the gifts that God is giving you for living out your personal ministry.

- You and members of your group will grow together as a Christian community and gain skills in learning how small groups in the church become settings for spiritual guidance.

A spiritual formation group encourages individuals to focus on deep questions such as:

How is God working in my life?

How am I being formed in the likeness of Christ?

What practices will open me to God's leading?

A spiritual formation group provides ways for you to open yourself to the Spirit.

A spiritual formation group helps you listen to the "still small voice" of God.

A spiritual formation group is a community marked by gratitude for the surprising ways God works in our lives and in the world.

A spiritual formation group honors each person's sharing, refrains from fixing or solving problems, and trusts the Spirit to guide each one.

A spiritual formation group is an adventure of growing and maturing in your faith.

Forming a Core Group for Promotion

Pray for a couple of people who will help you promote, plan, and initiate *Companions in Christ* in your church. Here are some questions to help you:

- Whom do you see as leaders in prayer in your congregation?
- Are there people who have been through an Academy for Spiritual Formation?
- Are there people who have gone through a spiritual-renewal experience such as Walk to Emmaus or Cursillo?
- Do you know of people in the congregation who have gone on one or more spiritual formation retreats?
- Is there a leader of prayer or spirituality among the women's or men's groups of your congregation?
- Could the church staff suggest several people who might become members of a prayer and planning group?
- Is there a spiritual formation committee in the church?

Invite two or three others from the above list to work with you in praying for and planning for *Companions in Christ*.

- Use "A Prayer for Recruiting" on page 214 or other prayers to place this program before God and the church.
- Discuss ways to promote *Companions in Christ*. Make use of the suggestions and resources in this book.
- List the names of people you wish to invite to participate.
- Coordinate your planning with the church staff and any other appropriate groups in your congregation.
- Make personal calls and send personal letters to those who might be interested. This guide includes sample letters.
- Pray for God's guidance.

Ideas for Promoting Companions in Christ

A sk someone to give a testimony during a Sunday morning worship service about his or her experience with prayer and invite the congregation to deepen its walk with God through *Companions in Christ*.

Hang a *Companions in Christ* flyer/poster in a prominent place in your church. This book includes two sample posters. The *Companions in Christ* Church Pack includes two four-color printed posters. These are also available free by calling The Upper Room and asking for M106 (telephone 1-800-972-0433).

Use the prayers on pages 214 and 218 in meetings, classes, and worship.

Hold an information meeting. This Getting Started Guide includes an outline for such a meeting.

Visit Sunday school classes, women's and men's groups, and any other small groups in your church to talk about *Companions in Christ*.

Mail an invitation to members of the congregation you think would be interested in a spiritual formation group. Follow up with phone calls.

Write a newsletter article about *Companions in Christ* or a series of articles that will generate ongoing interest.

Prepare and use a bulletin insert. Use the ideas in this *Getting Started Guide*.

Set up a display table with the Participant's Book, information about *Companions in Christ*, and some of the resource books.

Create a bulletin board with information about *Companions in Christ*.

Duplicate testimonials from other group participants that are printed on the *Companions in Christ* minicatalog or download them from the *Companions* Web site.

Finding a Leader for Companions in Christ

QUALITIES OR EXPERIENCES TO LOOK FOR

A person steeped in prayer. One who is familiar with a variety of ways of prayer and has a well-developed life of prayer;

A person who knows not only information about the Bible but is also familiar with the ways the Bible shapes and forms faith;

A person who is comfortable with silence, who doesn't have to answer every question, fill every silence;

A person who has experienced groups as a place for sharing, caring, and growth;

A person who is comfortable with differences and is able to be accepting of people at different stages of faith;

A person who can genuinely listen and who is attentive to the movements of the Spirit.

WHERE TO FIND A LEADER

To whom do people in the congregation go for help in prayer or for guidance in making decisions?

Who has shown leadership ability in other small-group settings? Has anyone been involved with the Academy for Spiritual Formation, Disciple, Emmaus, Cursillo?

Who has exhibited hunger for spiritual growth by asking questions, attending classes, going on retreats?

Just a Closer Walk?

Are you yearning for a deeper experience of God?

Would you like to be part of a small group
of people with whom you can share
questions of faith?

Come walk with

COMPANIONS *in Christ*

- A journey in prayer, scripture, sharing, spiritual friendship, and meditation.

- A spiritual-formation group designed to deepen your spiritual growth.

- An invitation from God to come close.

For more information, contact:

RESTLESS?
SEARCHING?

If you experience a spiritual hunger . . .

If you desire to bring a deeper dimension
to your faith . . .

we invite you to

COMPANIONS *in Christ*

A new small group that will provide support for your search.

A path to explore prayer, scripture, and the spiritual journey.

An experience of God's grace and love in daily times of
reflection.

Contact:

Creating a Companions in Christ Bulletin Board

Copy the cover of the Participant's Book.

Use the posters and fliers in this Guide.

Copy "What Is *Companions in Christ*?" from page 198.

List the time, date, and place for the beginning of *Companions in Christ*.

Feature some quotes on spiritual formation. This Guide provides several.

Put up the name of the contact person(s) with phone numbers.

Use the image of footsteps or a path to emphasize the spiritual journey.

Write in bold letters the following (the five study areas in *Companions in Christ*):
    Spiritual Journey
    Prayer
    Scripture
    Vocation and Gifts
    Spiritual Friendship

Include a sign-up list.

Use photographs, pictures, or images of people praying or reading the Bible or meeting in small groups or groups of people involved in common activities of discussion or outreach.

Deepen Your Prayer
Pray with Scripture
Identify Your Spiritual Gifts
Become a Spiritual Friend

It is all part of
Companions in Christ
A new small group opportunity that is beginning here on

_____

We invite you to become part of *Companions in Christ*, a small-group journey that focuses on deepening your relationship with God. Through daily readings, reflection, and weekly meetings, you will be guided in exploring prayer, scripture, vocation, and spiritual friendship as avenues to deepen your faith.

We promise that it will make a difference in your life.

For information, contact

_____

[or]

For information, see the display in the fellowship hall.

[or]

For information, come to the information meeting on

_____

[or]

For information, see the bulletin board.

(Adapt this last part as it best fits your congregation and your promotion.)

An Invitation to Sign Up
for Companions in Christ

Companions in Christ is

- A small group committed to deepening prayer and listening for the Spirit.

- Individuals who study each day about prayer, scripture, and discernment, and who keep a personal notebook or journal of their learnings and questions.

- A small group of people that meets weekly to support one another, share about what God is revealing in their reflections, and open themselves to exploring on a deeper level the theme of the week.

- Individuals who know that daily spiritual disciplines and weekly meetings offer a good balance and provide holy ground for growing in faith.

  If you wish to develop your daily disciplines and long for a small group with which to share the journey of faith, then come join *Companions in Christ*. For twenty-eight weeks, you will journey in a small group and be enriched, challenged, supported, and loved.

Will you accept?
If yes, sign below and we will contact you about the formation of the group.

Name _____

Address _____

Phone _____ E-mail _____

Name _____

Address _____

Phone _____ E-mail _____

(Use an invitation like this on a bulletin board or display table.)

For a Presentation about Companions in Christ and Its Five Gifts

O ne way to promote interest in *Companions in Christ* is to present the study to various church groups. Consider your congregation and choose groups that may have people who are interested in spiritual formation. Look at Sunday school classes, women's groups, prayer groups, men's groups, fellowship and study groups.

You may shape your presentation using the material in this Guide with an emphasis on the two components:
1. the daily readings and exercises and
2. the weekly small group for sharing and deepening the journey.

Or you may use this material on the gifts of *Companions in Christ*. As a visual, you may wish to gift wrap five boxes that you then unwrap as you talk about the five gifts.

FIRST GIFT: SPIRITUAL PRACTICES OR DISCIPLINES

Many people struggle with developing a daily time of prayer, scripture reading, meditation, and reflection. We know the longing to grow closer to God; and we know that prayer and silence, scripture and reflection are time-tested ways to open ourselves up to the movement of the Holy Spirit. Yet the busyness of life crowds in on us, and we do not follow through on our intentions.

> Spiritual growth is honed and perfected only through practice. Like an instrument, it must be played. Like a path, it must be walked. Whether through prayer or meditation or worship or good works, you must move yourself in the direction of spiritual betterment. Spiritual understanding never becomes deep unless you subject yourself to the spiritual discipline of practicing your belief.
>
> —Kent Nerburn, *Simple Truths*
> Novato, Calif.: New World Library, 1996, 93

Companions in Christ will give you a guide and a community to help you develop your spiritual practices. The guide will come in the form of your Participant's Book. Each day offers a reading or an exercise that takes about thirty minutes. The exercises will help you develop ways of prayer and meditation, inviting you into silence and reflection as well as reading and praying with the Bible. Your faithfulness to the thirty minutes each day will help pattern your life. Once you have established that daily pattern of prayer and reflection, you will discover that you can find the time to do it, and you will see the fruits of giving God that time each day.

You also will have a community to help, support, and challenge you. The members of this group will expect you faithfully to set aside time for prayer, daily exercises, and reflection. They can offer suggestions as to what works for them. They will pray for you to develop your own spiritual disciplines. You can trust there will be abundant grace when you have a bad week, and a measure of gentle, encouraging grace to keep you on the journey to a deeper walk with God and to developing your own spiritual practices.

SECOND GIFT: JOURNALING—KEEPING A PERSONAL NOTEBOOK

This may be a hard gift for some. Writing often does not come easily, and you can be so critical about what you write. With a busy schedule, you may find it difficult to make time to journal or you may resist putting what you think and feel into words on paper (or on a computer screen).

Yet journaling is one of the gifts of *Companions in Christ* and one of the gifts of the spiritual life. Writing is an inward and outward experience. It connects the world inside your mind and heart with a world that is larger than your thoughts. Putting words on paper and sharing them with others connects your inner prayer with the prayer of a community. This type of written reflection can help us understand our struggles. Putting your experiences and feelings into words helps you reflect on your relationship with God.

Journaling is also a way to record or keep track of what God is doing in your life. Over a period of time you may notice some common themes that reappear—God may be trying to get your attention. Or you may notice that you are not where you started. You may have forgotten to give thanks for the new place to which God has brought you. A personal journal becomes a gift for learning and gratitude.

Your journal is for your eyes only. You do not have to write complete sentences or full paragraphs or have perfect punctuation. It is meant for you to write your responses to the daily exercises. If you enter more into reflection and worry less about style or form, you will move toward perceiving journaling as one of your companions on the spiritual journey.

You will be invited to write prayers, write about your experiences, wrestle with new ideas, write to God and about God. Such variety of exercises will open you to the possibilities of continuing with the practice of journaling.

At weekly meetings, the participants will have time to talk about their responses to the daily exercises. You can decide what and how much you wish to share of your personal reflections.

> Journaling can be a significant tool in deepening our spiritual lives because by its nature it leads us to further revelation of who we are and who God is in our lives.
>
> —Anne Broyles, *Journaling: A Spiritual Journey*
> Nashville, Tenn.: Upper Room Books, 1999, 11.

THIRD GIFT: READING SCRIPTURE FOR FORMATION

Most Christians are familiar with Bible study. In many churches, substantial Bible studies such as Kerygma, Bethel, and Disciple Bible Study have had a profound and lasting effect on many people. We commend Bible study to you.

In *Companions in Christ*, the concern is not so much with information about the who, when, and why of the Bible as with letting scripture form you. "Let the same mind be in you that was in Christ Jesus" (Phil. 2:5). You read scripture to let the images and words shape you in the likeness of Christ. You want to do more than *think* about God's Word; you want to let that Word enter and transform you.

You will be introduced to several formational ways of reading scripture. One is the classic practice of *lectio divina*, which means holy or "divine reading." It is a slow, meditative, repetitive reading of scripture and letting a word or image from the passage descend to your heart and guide your prayer. You will learn, like Mary, to ponder these things deeply in your heart (Luke 2:19).

You will also be invited to use your imagination in reading scripture. This approach works particularly well with narrative or story portions of scripture as you imagine yourself back in the text with Jesus and Zacchaeus or on the road to Emmaus. Entering into the story with your imagination frees God to reveal new insights and truths.

You will read scripture with new eyes.

> God's word will speak to us and transform our lives if we will come to it in a spirit of prayer and expectancy. The invitation is for us to seek the living presence of God in the Bible and to come ready to listen and respond.
>
> —E. Glenn Hinson, *Companions in Christ*, Participant's Book

FOURTH GIFT: SPIRITUAL FRIENDSHIP

This gift of *Companions in Christ* goes by many names. It is called spiritual direction, spiritual guidance, or spiritual friendship. Though there are differences, all of them involve another person with whom you can share your prayer life, your growing closer to God. You long to know if there is another who experiences what you experience, who can help you see the way to go or notice where you have been. You sometimes want someone to help you pay attention to the movements of the Holy Spirit in your life.

> I began to pray for someone who would guide me in the essential, formative parts of my life: my sense of God, my practice of prayer, my understanding of grace. I wanted someone who would take my life of prayer and my pilgrimage with Christ as seriously (or more seriously) than I did, who was capable of shutting up long enough to hear the distinct uniqueness of my spirituality, and who had enough disciplined restraint not to impose an outside form on me.
>
> —Eugene Peterson. *Working the Angles*
> Grand Rapids, Mich.: Eerdmans, 1987, 117.

An essential part of being a spiritual friend is the ability to listen. A spiritual friend, guide, or director does a lot of listening—listening for common themes, listening for hints of the Spirit, listening for openings to growth in closeness to God. It is a great gift to listen to another without worrying about what you will say, while learning to trust the Holy Spirit as the ultimate guide.

Spiritual guidance is not primarily about problem solving as is usually the case in therapy or counseling. Rather, spiritual guidance helps the person find God's hand or the Spirit's guidance in the midst of the issue. Spiritual guidance is not about theological instruction though a person may be invited to explore his or her image of God or enter into a meditative reading of scripture.

Companions in Christ will acquaint you with the practice of listening (some call it holy listening) for the movement of the Spirit and how to befriend another on their journey. You also will learn about and practice group spiritual guidance and patterns of discernment.

FIFTH GIFT: BEFRIENDING YOUR VOCATION

God calls you to be active in the world. For many people, the key question is, "Where can I get a good job that pays a lot of money?" *Companions in Christ* will invite you to ask different questions, to see that your "job" in the Christian tradition is an opportunity to explore what God would have you do in the world and how to use your God-given gifts.

Every Christian has been given a spiritual gift. Simply defined, spiritual gifts are particular abilities given by Christ through the Holy Spirit for the good of the whole church so it may do Christ's work in the world.

—Gerrit Scott Dawson, *Companions in Christ*, Participant's Book

You will be introduced to looking at your life through the gifts given by the Holy Spirit. You will be invited to identify your own gifts and also receive the wisdom of the group members as they name some gifts they see in you. Knowing and claiming your gifts enables you to see ways God might use you in the world.

A key part of this gift of befriending your vocation is to look at how the spiritual gifts given by God are meant not only for individuals and their careers but for use in building up the kingdom of God. You will also have a chance to reflect on what gifts the congregation has as it seeks to carry out its ministry and mission in the community and the world.

Recruiting

A Prayer for Recruiting

God of the heights and depths,
we open ourselves to an outpouring of your grace.
Move among us and place in your people a desire
to enter into a closer walk with you.
Set our hearts on fire with longing to dwell in your holy word
and deepen our prayer.

As we thirst for you, O God,
raise up a group who will be our companions in Christ
and be a witness to your presence in all of life
and especially in our community of faith.

God of the heights and depths,
bless our congregation with a new group of faithful disciples,
your companions on the way.
Amen.

Dear Friend(s),

A minister told of a church she served where people wanted Bible study. She would arrange wonderful studies with good teachers and advertise widely. Yet few people showed up, even though people consistently said they wanted Bible study. Finally it dawned on her that what people really wanted was not information about the Bible but an experience of God.

I think that is what we all want, to experience some intimacy with God, to have a deep relationship with Christ. Worship is a part of that journey to God and so is study. But one of the clearest paths to experiencing God is a small group that knows how to share and care, that values prayer and silence, that listens for the movement of the Spirit.

I want to invite you to become part of *Companions in Christ*—a new spiritual formation group that will provide ways and paths for you to grow closer to God. Through daily reading and reflections from your Participant's Book and with a weekly meeting with fellow companions, you will have created the space for God to draw near and abide with you.

To learn more about this opportunity, please talk to me or attend an information meeting on

I believe it will make a difference in your life and bring about renewal in the life of the congregation.

Your companion in Christ,

A letter of invitation to those who might be interested in Companions in Christ

Dear _____,

Thank you for your interest in *Companions in Christ*. I am glad that God has led you to inquire about participating. Here are the main components of this resource and some idea of what you would be committing yourself to:

1. Daily reading and reflecting

On the day after the group meeting, you would read the chapter for the coming week. For the next five days you would work on the daily exercises that invite your reflection, prayer, and exploration of the theme. Many of the exercises ask that you reflect on a scripture passage, so you will need your Bible. You will want to record your responses to questions, insights, and musings in a notebook or journal. Before you come to the weekly meetings, read through your journal to see the ways God has been at work in you. On an average, the daily reading and reflection may take thirty minutes. Sometimes the Spirit really stirs, and you will want to spend more time with the exercises.

2. Weekly meetings

The small group will gather for two hours each week. After a time of centering and worship, the first part of the meeting will be spent in sharing responses to the exercises. Bring your journal. There is not time for everyone to share all of his or her responses to the exercises, but it is expected that each person will have done all the daily work. Tell where you experienced God's speaking to you, where you have questions, where you believe God is leading. Also be prepared to listen for common themes that emerge in the sharing.

The second major component of the weekly meeting is time for "Deeper Explorations." This will expand on a part of the week's theme or offer further practice in spiritual exercises being taught in the unit. The leader will guide this portion and will appreciate your openness and willingness to participate. Bring your Bible as well as your journal to the weekly meetings.

The weekly meeting will close with perhaps a word about next week, but always with a time of prayer, worship, or song. Most group members share in prayer for one another, a wonderful gift we rarely offer face to face.

3. Openness

You agree to be open to God's leading through the readings, reflections, and the small-group experience. Having the sense of opening your hands and heart to God is an important way to begin this journey of allowing your life to be formed in the image of Christ.

I trust this gives you some idea of your commitment to this wonderful opportunity to be companions in Christ. I look forward to your registration and participation. If I can be of further assistance, please do call.

Another companion in Christ,

A letter of invitation to those who have expressed interest in Companions in Christ

Companions in Christ
Registration Form

Name _____

Address _____

Phone: Day _____ Night _____

Fax _____ E-mail _____ Birthday _____

❏ I would like to be part of *Companions in Christ*.

❏ I want more information on *Companions in Christ*.

My preferred meeting time for the weekly two-hour meeting is (check all that work for you):

❏ Sunday   ❏ Morning   ❏ Afternoon   ❏ Evening

❏ Monday   ❏ Morning   ❏ Afternoon   ❏ Evening

❏ Tuesday   ❏ Morning   ❏ Afternoon   ❏ Evening

❏ Wednesday ❏ Morning   ❏ Afternoon   ❏ Evening

❏ Thursday   ❏ Morning   ❏ Afternoon   ❏ Evening

❏ Friday   ❏ Morning   ❏ Afternoon   ❏ Evening

❏ Saturday   ❏ Morning   ❏ Afternoon   ❏ Evening

❏ I will need help with childcare.

Other concerns or special needs:

Candle Prayer

*U*se the following as an opening prayer for your information meeting and/or for each time *Companions in Christ* meets. Light a candle or several, and invite everyone to join in the prayer.

*L*ight of Christ

*S*hine on our path

*C*hase away all darkness

and lead us to the heart of God.

Amen.

Information Meeting Outline

Opening

- Light a candle and use the Candle Prayer (page 218)
- Sing a song or have a period of silence
- Pray this prayer:

  God of Love, embrace us in this sacred time and let our restless hearts find their rest in you. Move in our midst and open us to the possibilities for a closer walk with you. Thank you for these people who long to see your face. Bless our time together. Amen.

Welcome

Welcome all and express appreciation for their coming to this information meeting. God is always drawing us closer. Thank people for paying attention to the work of the Spirit.

Sharing

Invite people to share their names and what drew them to this meeting. If a large group shows up, you may want to do this exercise in smaller groups, later inviting each small group to present a summary report to the whole group.

Presentation/Information

Do an overview of *Companions in Christ* and speak on these points:

1. *Companions in Christ* is a small-group resource for spiritual formation. It focuses on experience: the experience of the participants as they study, pray, reflect, and share in the group; and the experience of the group members as they take their learnings into the church and community.

2. *Companions in Christ* has two main components:
   - Individual reading and daily exercises from the Participant's Book

- A weekly two-hour meeting to share responses to the weekly exercises and to explore at a deeper level the theme for the week, which is facilitated by a leader using the Leader's Guide.

3. Journaling will be introduced as the primary way to record and reflect on the movement of the Spirit in each person through the week and at the group session.

4. The five parts cover five major themes:

   - Embracing the Journey: The Way of Christ—looking at spirituality as a journey toward wholeness and holiness

   - Feeding on the Word: The Mind of Christ—an introduction to several ways of praying and meditating on Scripture

   - Deepening Our Prayer: The Heart of Christ—experiencing different ways of prayer

   - Responding to Our Call: The Work of Christ—looking at our vocation as Christians and the spiritual gifts we have to share

   - Exploring Spiritual Guidance: The Spirit of Christ—an overview of different ways of receiving and giving spiritual guidance as individuals or in groups

If you have the Participant's Book(s) and the Leader's Guide, you may wish to display them, inviting group members to peruse them at the meeting's conclusion.

A TIME OF LISTENING AND SHARING

Invite those present to experience the style of sharing that will be present in *Companions in Christ*. Suggest an amount of time in which to do the exercise that gives each person time to reflect, talk, and listen.

In twos or threes, reflect on a time you felt close to God. Spend a couple of minutes writing in a journal or notebook and then share with those who are in your group. Where was it? What did you experience? Was there any sense that God wanted you do something?

INVITATION

Invite commitment to entering the *Companions in Christ* group.

Have a sign-up sheet that persons may sign or copies of the registration form found in this book. Talk about when you will begin *Companions in Christ* if that has been decided and if appropriate.

CLOSING SONG AND PRAYER

Supporting

Training Events

To lead a small group through the formational process of *Companions in Christ* effectively, a leader will benefit from having a clear understanding of the resource and a basic experience of the process embodied in the resource. Leaders will also benefit from developing some distinctive leadership skills. Leading formational groups calls for skills such as listening, patience, accepting differences, and working with process more than content. Upper Room Ministries offers one-day and three-day training events for leaders of *Companions in Christ*. While training is not mandatory, we strongly recommend that you attend a training event, especially if your experience with formational small groups or spiritual practice is limited.

Both the one-day and three-day training events will provide guidance for leaders in the following areas:

- Understanding the *Companions in Christ* vision

- Experiencing various aspects of *Companions in Christ*

- Using ongoing leadership support through the *Companions in Christ* Network

- Implementing the process in local congregations

Leader Orientations are basic one-day training events offered around the country. In addition to the areas mentioned above, the Leader Orientations will offer basic training in leadership qualities and skills for leading spiritual formation groups.

Leader Trainings are advanced three-day events. In addition to the above areas, the Leader Trainings will provide advanced training in the leadership qualities and skills for leading spiritual formation groups (including practice in guiding the small-group process).

For additional information about dates and locations of Leader Orientations or Leader Trainings, see the *Companions in Christ* Web page (www.companionsinchrist.org) or contact Upper Room Ministries at 1-800-972-0433.

Sustaining a Spiritual Formation Group

The circumstances and details of daily life can impact each individual as well as the whole of a small group. Some events cannot be anticipated or prevented, but there are ways to help sustain the group over the course of many weeks.

1. Pray for the group members.

   As a leader or a member of *Companions in Christ*, remember one another in prayer.

2. Communicate the schedule clearly.

   Make sure everyone knows about changes in meeting dates or in assignments.

3. Make calls, and send cards.

   If a person misses a meeting, ask someone in the group to call. You may wish to save handouts for that person and ask one participant to provide a summary of what happened. Groups may also remember the person by lighting a candle during the meeting. If a person misses several of the group sessions, a call and a card from the leader is appropriate. If your group is small, try to check in with members during the week.

4. Observe group process.

   Make sure all participants have a chance to share, that no one monopolizes the conversations or tries to fix someone else's problem. The Leader's Guide contains more information on small-group process and the Leader Training Events will provide experiential help with small-group dynamics.

5. Pray in the meeting room.

   As you set up for each meeting, offer a prayer for all who will enter that holy space. Bernard of Clairvaux once said, "God loves both more than you and before you." Pray that in this space the group will discover the reality of God who is already here.

6. Check in with the group.

   Do participants need vacation or holiday breaks? a coffee/refreshment/meal after each meeting? Would a field trip to a retreat center or some special worship experience be helpful? Would a social gathering to strengthen the bonds of community beyond the weekly meetings be important to schedule? Is there a time to invite other family members for a social evening or gathering?

7. Plan the environment.

   Comfortable chairs and a small table are important aspects of setting up the meeting space. Consider displaying art and pictures in the room and developing a visual focus for the table. Flowers, tablecloths, candles, or thematic symbols can help people enter into the sharing. Music to sing and music for meditation are also essential elements.

8. Consider prayer partners.

   At each meeting, each participant could draw the name of another group member. That person would be his or her special prayer focus for the coming week. Or participants could draw a name for each unit of study, remembering that person and her or his prayer requests for five to six weeks.

9. Planning

   Circumstances or life patterns may cause some persons to show up late for the beginning of the meeting. Conversations, insights, or concerns may cause a meeting to go longer than the two hours. Therefore the leader needs to plan carefully for the various time blocks in each meeting and be prepared to adjust as necessary.

   Above all, to help the group be faithful to the two-hour meeting, the leader should stress the importance of a covenant of expectations.

Congregational Prayer Support

As a *Companions in Christ* group forms in the congregation, invite the congregation into prayerful support.

- Invite the congregation to pray for the group's initial formation.

- Publish "A Prayer for Recruiting" in your church bulletin and church newsletter.

- Develop a "church breath prayer"—a short sentence prayer focused on the new group. You could create your own or use one of these:

   "Holy God, call us forth to walk with you."

   "Loving God, raise from among us companions in Christ."

- Enlist members of the congregation who are not involved in the study to pray whenever the group meets. This ministry allows housebound or shut-in persons to play an active part.

Linking Up with Other Companions

*A*n additional dimension of *Companions in Christ* is the network. While your group is experiencing *Companions*, groups in other congregations also will be meeting. By providing a Web site (www.companionsinchrist.org), The Upper Room will establish a network link among the *Companions in Christ* groups. The network provides opportunities for groups to share their experiences with one another and to communicate in a variety of meaningful ways. As you move through the resource, there will be occasions when you are asked to pray for another group, send greetings or words of encouragement, or receive their support for your group. You may discover that your group will find additional ways it wants to relate to other *Companions in Christ* groups. We encourage you to do so and to share your experiences. Here are some ideas:

Visit www.companionsinchrist.org and encourage members of your group to do likewise.

From the Web, print out the list of other *Companions* groups and bring it to your group meeting. Decide if you want to select a *Companions* group from another congregation to be your partner. If you decide to partner with another group, consider the benefits of partnering with a group that is geographically close or distant.

Pray for your *Companions* partner group.

Send letters of encouragement to them.

Make or purchase small, inexpensive gifts to send to your partner group.

Take a photo of your group and include it in a card to your *Companions* partner group.

If geographically close, ask your partner group to share a special activity with you, such as providing gifts for a needy family at Christmas or joining in a summer mission project.

Introduce your *Companions* partner group to the rest of your congregation through your church newsletter or bulletin inserts.

Visit the *Companions* discussion room on the Web site. Let other groups benefit from your learnings and experiences or offer testimonies from your group.

Discover what ministries you share with your *Companions* partner group.

If the Leader Must Miss a Weekly Meeting

- Choose a group member to lead the session. Meet with that member and supply a copy of all appropriate material from the Leader's Guide. Go over the general outline of the session, including the time for reflecting on weekly exercises and the time for the deeper exploration of the theme. Give special attention to preparation details such as set-up, materials, and handouts.

- Another possibility is to ask two members to share leadership. One could do the opening worship and sharing on the exercises, while the other leads the deeper explorations and closing worship. In this case, the two would need to work closely on set-up and preparation details.

- If no one can lead the group, adjust the schedule until the leader returns.

Resources

A Possible Schedule for the 28-Week Experience

Second week of September	Preparatory Meeting
Third week of September	Embracing the Journey 1
Fourth week of September	Embracing the Journey 2
First week of October	Embracing the Journey 3
Second week of October	Embracing the Journey 4
Third week of October	Embracing the Journey 5
Fourth week of October	Feeding on the Word 1
First week of November	Feeding on the Word 2
Second week of November	Feeding on the Word 3
Third week of November	Feeding on the Word 4
Fourth week of November	Thanksgiving Break
First week of December	Feeding on the Word 5
Christmas break	1–4 weeks

(If you started after the second week of September, you could do one or two more sessions before Christmas. Also if it fits your schedule better, you could begin the next part—Deepening our Prayer)

First week of January	Deepening Our Prayer 1
Second week of January	Deepening Our Prayer 2
Third week of January	Deepening Our Prayer 3
Fourth week of January	Deepening Our Prayer 4
First week of February	Deepening Our Prayer 5
Second week of February	Deepening Our Prayer 6
Third week of February	Responding to Our Call 1

Fourth week of February	Responding to Our Call 2
First week of March	Responding to Our Call 3
Second week of March	Responding to Our Call 4
Third week of March	Responding to Our Call 5
Fourth week of March	Exploring Spiritual Guidance 1
Easter Break	

(Depending on the date of Easter, you may wish to postpone beginning the fifth part on Exploring Spiritual Guidance until after Easter. If Easter is late, you may be able to finish most of the unit before Easter. Be conscious of school vacation schedules)

Second week of April	Exploring Spiritual Guidance 2
Third week of April	Exploring Spiritual Guidance 3
Fourth week of April	Exploring Spiritual Guidance 4
First week of May	Exploring Spiritual Guidance 5
Second week of May	A Closing Retreat

Tailor the schedule to your group's church and community circumstances. You may wish to take a break between each part (though it is recommended that you do not take a break between Parts 1 and 2 as the group is just beginning its formation) as well as taking breaks for the holidays.

A List of
Group Participants

Name _____

Address _____

Home phone _____ Work phone _____

E-mail _____

Name _____

Address _____

Home phone _____ Work phone _____

E-mail _____

Name _____

Address _____

Home phone _____ Work phone _____

E-mail _____

Name _____

Address _____

Home phone _____ Work phone _____

E-mail _____

Name _____

Address _____

Home phone _____ Work phone _____

E-mail _____

Recommended Bibles

The Spiritual Formation Bible: Growing in Intimacy with God through Scripture

New Revised Standard Version (NRSV). Available from Upper Room Books Customer Service, PO Box 340012 Nashville, TN 37203-9540 or call 1-800-972-0433. This Bible feature articles on spiritual formation, quotes, and meditations on each page that suggest ways to let scripture guide your prayer and life. Introductory notes and articles on spiritual disciplines make this a valuable tool for spiritual growth and an especially appropriate Bible for use with *Companions in Christ*.

New Interpreter's Study Bible

New Revised Standard Version with Apocrypha. Extensive notes on text, guides for interpretation, glossary, chronologies, and maps make this a helpful study guide. Published by Abingdon Press.

Oxford Annotated Study Bible

This Bible has annotations and explanatory notes on each page, introductions to every book of the Bible, and a full set of New Oxford Bible maps. New Revised Standard Version.

Harper Collins Study Bible

Contains verse-by-verse annotation of key words or phrases, and offers cross-references to other passages.

The Access Bible

A New Revised Standard Version that features running commentary interspersed with the biblical text. In-text maps, charts, and sidebar essays provide extensive background information.

Helpful Background Resources

A more expanded resource list is found in the Participant's Book(s).

Jones, W. Paul. *The Art of Spiritual Direction: Giving and Receiving Spiritual Guidance.* What is spiritual direction? What is the difference between spiritual direction and counseling? How can you know if you are called to the ministry of spiritual direction? What should happen in spiritual direction sessions? Jones answers these and other questions in this overview of spiritual direction.

Miller, Wendy J. *Jesus, Our Spiritual Director: A Pilgrimage through the Gospels* (#9876). The reader encounters Jesus as personal spiritual guide and also learns how to encourage others in their sacred journey through life. Wendy Miller brings the Gospel texts to life as a continuing conversation between Jesus and his disciples then and now. She demonstrates the deep biblical roots of spiritual direction.

Morris, Robert Corin. *Wrestling with Grace: A Spirituality for the Rough Edges of Daily Life.* Morris offers liberating news to anyone who longs for everyday spiritual practice. He nudges us toward new ways of looking at our own behavior and state of mind, showing us how to let God's grace into daily life. Ten prayer exercises at the end of the book provide ongoing guidance for searchers.

Mulholland Jr., M. Robert. *Shaped by the Word: The Power of Scripture in Spiritual Formation*, revised. Nashville, Tenn.: Upper Room Books, 2000. An exploration of using scripture as a guide to prayer and spiritual formation.

Steere, Douglas V. *Dimensions of Prayer: Cultivating a Relationship with God*, revised. Nashville, Tenn.: Upper Room Books, 2002. A classic work that inspires and educates people on deepening their prayer life.

Thompson, Marjorie. *Soul Feast: An Invitation to the Christian Spiritual Life.* Louisville, Ky.: Westminster John Knox Press, 2005. A good introduction to the basic spiritual disciplines that are part of *Companions in Christ.* It could also serve as a preparatory study resource for a group before members begin the more in-depth commitment of *Companions in Christ.*

Vest, Norvene. *Gathered in the Word: Praying the Scripture in Small Groups.* Nashville, Tenn.: Upper Room Books, 1996. Vest describes an age-old form of devotional reading intended specifically for spiritual nourishment, called *lectio divina.*

Wolpert, Daniel. *Creating a Life with God: The Call of Ancient Prayer Practices.* Nashville, Tenn.: Upper Room Books, 2003. A basic resource that offers the opportunity to learn and adopt 12 prayer practices.

Quotes

The hunger of the heart is. . . . always a beginning. Either it is an opportunity to let God into our lives for the first time, or it is a chance to move further along the path of spiritual growth with God at our side.

—Ron DelBene
The Hunger of the Heart, A Workbook (Nashville, Tenn.: Upper Room Books, 1995), 16.

Whether you like it or no, read and pray daily. It is for your life; there is no other way: else you will be trifler all your days. . . . Do justice to your own soul; give it time and means to grow. Do not starve yourself any longer.

—John Wesley
John Wesley and Modern Religion, Umphrey Lee
(Nashville, Tenn.: Cokesbury, 1936), 107–8

All your love, your stretching out, your hope, your thirst, God is creating in you so that [God] may fill you. . . . God is on the inside of the longing.

—Maria Boulding
The Coming of God
(Collegeville, Maine: Liturgical Press, 1986), 167

Next Steps

Suggested Next Steps

When the group completes the twenty-eight-week journey of *Companions in Christ*, participants may wonder what to do next. Here are some suggestions. Trust the Spirit to open new possibilities and trust the Spirit to lead the group participants to a new sense of call and discernment.

- Nurture anyone who feels called to lead another group of *Companions in Christ*. It is possible to have several spiritual formation groups going at the same time. Some of those who have been through the journey may now be ready to lead a group. Others may wish to participate in the *Companions in Christ* training and then begin a group.

- After completing Part 4 on vocation and gifts, some group members may have a greater clarity as to a new ministry they want to begin or be involved in. Provide support and encouragement.

- New ministries of prayer could develop at the completion of *Companions in Christ*: a prayer support group, a group committed to intercession, a group that meets for silence and contemplation, a Covenant Discipleship group.

- A group of people who would like to continue meditating weekly on scripture, perhaps using the lectionary readings as a basis for "Group *Lectio*" (see Part 2, week 5) or using directed imagination (Part 2, week 4) could emerge.

- A group may wish to explore the annotated resource list found in the back of the Participant's Book(s). This list offers additional small group and individual resources that expand on the themes of the five parts.

- A worship experience that uses the meditative approach to scripture could be offered.

- Persons may be led to seek further training in spiritual direction. Contact Spiritual Directors International, PO Box 3584, Bellevue, WA 98009-3584. Phone: 425-455-1565. E-mail presence@sdiworld.org for a list of training programs.

- With guidance from the participants in *Companions in Christ*, the church could establish a program of prayer partners.

Evaluation

When your group has completed the *Companions in Christ* closing retreat, please share your insights and experiences in relation to the questions below. Use additional paper if needed. (If you are evaluating one of the parts of the Companions in Christ resource, use the evaluation sheet at the back of the individual Participant's Books.)

1. Describe your group's experience with *Companions in Christ*.

2. How could *Companions in Christ* be improved either overall or in any component?

3. Do you have follow-up plans for your group? What resource do you plan to use, or what kinds of resources are you looking for?

Mail to: *Companions in Christ*
            Upper Room Ministries
            P. O. Box 340004
            Nashville, TN 37203-0012
Or email: companions@upperroom.org

Supplemental Music Resources

*S*uggestions have been supplied in each week of the Leader's Guide for hymn/song options in the Opening and Closing worship times of the group meeting. We trust that as a leader of the group you will freely explore your own church hymnals and songbooks with an eye to lyrics that fit the weekly subject. You have great latitude to select music that fits your context and group environment. Naturally, we encourage you to draw on the gifts of any persons with musical ability in the group.

Recognizing that each group is likely to have its own preference in musical style and that congregational hymnals and songbooks vary significantly in content, we offer the following list of supplementary songs to encourage a broader repertoire of music for weekly meetings. This list draws on commonly used contemporary praise music, newer hymnody that supplements standard hymnals, and some selections of music from the Taizé and Iona Communities that are gaining in appeal among Christians worldwide. (For ordering information about Taizé and Iona music resources, contact GIA Publications, Inc., 7404 S. Mason Ave., Chicago, Illinois 60638-9927 or call 800-GIA-1358.) In a small group, many of these selections would work best with accompaniment. If your group has someone who plays piano, guitar, or autoharp and you have access to such instruments, we particularly encourage your exploration of these resources. If you have no potential accompanists, you might consider the use of music audiocassettes or CDs. Some pieces are simple enough to teach a group for unaccompanied singing.

The music listed on the next pages can be found in the following primary resources (abbreviations indicated):

- *The Faith We Sing*, a supplement to *The United Methodist Hymnal*. Nashville, Tenn.: Abingdon Press, 2000. (TFWS)

- *Praise: Maranatha Music Chorus Book*. Expanded 2nd Ed. Maranatha Music, 1990. (MP)

- *Renew! Songs and Hymns for Blended Worship*. Robert Webber, ed. Carol Stream, Ill.: Hope Publishing, 1995.(RENEW)

- *The Upper Room Worshipbook*. Nashville, Tenn.: The Upper Room, June, 2006. (URW)

These selections are organized under the five parts of *Companions in Christ* and by weeks within the first part. Numerous options are listed for Part 1, but many of these songs would fit well with the weekly themes of later parts. Rather than listing them again, we suggest that you notice the songs your group responds to with appreciation and keep track of music that might be sung again in later weeks.

PREPARATORY MEETING

Jesus, Stand among Us	(RENEW)
Prepare the Way (Taizé)	(RENEW)
One Thing Have I Desired	(MP)

PART 1: EMBRACING THE JOURNEY: THE WAY OF CHRIST

Christian Life as Journey (Week 1)

In the Morning I Will Sing	(URW)
We Are Marching	(TFWS)
Lead Me, Lord	(RENEW)
I Have Decided to Follow Jesus	(TFWS)
Seekers of Your Heart	(MP)
I Was There to Hear Your Borning Cry	(TFWS)

The Nature of the Christian Life (Week 2)

God Claims You	(TFWS)
Behold, What Manner of Love	(MP)
In His Presence	(MP)
God Is So Good	(TFWS)

The Flow and the Means of Grace (Week 3)

Sanctuary	(TFWS)
Grace Alone	(TFWS)
O How He Loves You and Me	(TFWS)
More like You	(TFWS)
O Lord, Your Tenderness	(RENEW)

Sharing Journeys of Faith (Week 4)

Bless the Lord, My Soul (Taizé)	(URW, TFWS)
Bless the Lord, O My Soul (Crouch)	(TFWS)
I Want to Walk as a Child of the Light	(RENEW)
Just a Closer Walk with Thee	(TFWS)
If It Had Not Been for the Lord	(TFWS)

Living as Covenant Community (Week 5)

Gather Us In (Here in This Place)	(TFWS)
We Are One in the Bond of Love	(Hymns for the Family of God)
There Is One Lord (Taizé)	(RENEW)
They'll Know We are Christians by Our Love	(TFWS)
O Look and Wonder	(TFWS)
Let Us Be Bread	(TFWS)
Let There Be Love	(MP)
Praise to You, O God of Mercy	(RENEW)
You Are My Hiding Place	(TFWS)
Weave	(URW)

General Closing Songs

God to Enfold You (Iona)	(URW)
May You Run and Not Be Weary	(TFWS)
You Shall Go Out with Joy	(URW, TFWS)

PART 2: FEEDING ON THE WORD: THE MIND OF CHRIST

Change My Heart, O God	(TFWS)
More Like You	(TFWS)

PART 3: DEEPENING OUR PRAYER: THE HEART OF CHRIST

Hear, O Lord	(MP)
I'm So Glad Jesus Lifted Me	(TFWS)
In His Time	(TFWS)
Without Seeing You	(TFWS)
Turn Your Eyes Upon Jesus	(MP)

PART 4: RESPONDING TO OUR CALL: THE WORK OF CHRIST

Christ in Me	(MP)
Living for Jesus	(TFWS)
Love, Love (round)	(MP)
Freely, Freely	(RENEW)
Give Me a Clean Heart	(TFWS)
Together We Serve	(TFWS)
Take, O Take (Iona)	(URW)

PART 5: EXPLORING SPIRITUAL GUIDANCE: THE SPIRIT OF CHRIST

The Trees of the Field	(URW, TFWS)
We Must Wait (on the Lord)	(MP)

CLOSING RETREAT

Bind Us Together	(TFWS)
O Look and Wonder	(TFWS)

Notes

PART 1

Week 2
1. Henri J. M. Nouwen, excerpt from a lecture at Scarritt-Bennett Center, February 8, 1991.
2. Janet Wolf, "Chosen for…," *Upper Room Disciplines 1999* (Nashville, Tenn.: Upper Room Books, 1999), 128.

Week 3
1. *Encounter with God's Love: Selected Writings of Julian of Norwich* (Nashville, Tenn.: Upper Room Books, 1998), 16.
2. Saint Augustine, *Confessions*, trans. R. S. Pine-Coffin (Harmondsworth, England: Penguin Books, 1961),177–78.
3. *A Longing for Holiness: Selected Writings of John Wesley,* ed. Keith Beasley-Topliffe (Nashville, Tenn.: Upper Room Books, 1997), 35–37.

Week 5
1. Dietrich Bonhoeffer, *Life Together* (San Francisco: HarperSanFrancisco, 1954), 77.

PART 2

Week 1
1. M. Robert Mulholland Jr., *Shaped by the Word: The Power of Scripture in Spiritual Formation*, rev. ed. (Nashville, Tenn.: The Upper Room, 2000), 43.

PART 3

Week 1
1. Brother Lawrence, *The Practice of the Presence of God,* trans. Robert J. Edmonson (Orleans, Mass.: Paraclete Press, 1985), 93. Brother Lawrence was a lay Carmelite of the seventeenth century whose writings on "practicing God's presence" have been cherished by Christians of all traditions in the intervening centuries.

Week 2

1. Bonhoeffer, *Life Together*, 84.
2. Ibid.
3. Richard of Chichester, from *A Book of Personal Prayer*, comp. René O. Bideaux (Nashville, Tenn.: Upper Room Books, 1997), 21.

PART 4

Week 1

1. Eugene H. Peterson, *The Message* (Colorado Springs, Col.: NavPress, 1993), 145.

Week 2

1. Beth Richardson, "The Broken Places," *alive now!* (May–June 1991), 15.
2. Henri J. M. Nouwen, *The Wounded Healer* (New York: Image Books, 1979), 94.

Week 3

1. The foot-washing service is an adaptation of one described in the book *Heartfelt: Finding Our Way Back to God* by Gerrit Scott Dawson (Nashville, Tenn.: Upper Room Books, 1993), 106–7.

PART 5

Week 1

1. Thomas N. Hart, *The Art of Christian Listening* (New York: Paulist Press, 1980), 32.
2. Eugene H. Peterson, *Working the Angles: The Shape of Pastoral Integrity* (Grand Rapids, Mich.: William B. Eerdmans, 1987), 103–4.

About the Authors

Stephen D. Bryant is the World Editor and Publisher, Upper Room Ministries

Janice T. Grana is former World Editor and Publisher, Upper Room Ministries and former Executive Editor, Upper Room Books

Marjorie J. Thompson is the Director of the Pathways Center for Congregational Spirituality, Upper Room Ministries

Prayers for Our COMPANIONS *in Christ* Group

W e sign this card to indicate our desire to be *lifted in prayer* and to add our group's name to the listing on the website as we continue our *Companions in Christ* journey. Or you may enter your Companions group information at www.companionsinchrist.org/leaders. This ministry of prayer for *Companions in Christ* groups is an offering of The Upper Room Living Prayer Center and its numerous covenant prayer groups across the country. These prayer groups have made a covenant to lift us as individuals and as a group in prayer once our card is received.

Leader Name: _____

Leader Email: _____

Church Name: _____

Church Address: _____

City/State/Zip: _____

Church Email: _____

All members are invited to sign their first name below.

Please include your return address:

_____

_____

_____

BUSINESS REPLY MAIL
FIRST-CLASS MAIL PERMIT NO. 1540 NASHVILLE TN

POSTAGE WILL BE PAID BY ADDRESSEE

COMPANIONS in Christ

UPPER ROOM MINISTRIES
PO BOX 340012
NASHVILLE, TN 37203-9540